Skinny Ninnie's Kitchen

Skinny Ninnie's Kitchen

— RECIPES & HUMOR —

FROM FOUR GENERATIONS OF SOUTHERN MOUTHS

Autumn Beck Blackledge

Copyright © 2018 by Autumn Beck Blackledge

All rights reserved. No portion of this publication may be reproduced, stored in a retrieval system, or transmitted by any means-electronic, mechanical, photocopying, recording, or any other-except for brief quotations in printed reviews, without the prior written permission of the publisher.

Indigo River Publishing
3 West Garden Street Ste. 352
Pensacola, FL 32502
www.indigoriverpublishing.com

Ordering Information:
Quantity sales: Special discounts are available on quantity purchases by corporations, associations, and others. For details, contact the publisher at the address above.

Orders by U.S. trade bookstores and wholesalers: Please contact the publisher at the address above.

Printed in the United States of America

Editor: Regina Cornell
Book Design: mycustombookcover.com
Project Manager: Stephen Rampersad

Library of Congress Control Number: 2018942678
ISBN: 978-1-948080-25-5

First Edition

With Indigo River Publishing, you can always expect great books, strong voices, and meaningful messages. Most importantly, you'll always find … words worth reading.

FAMILY PHOTO: *Ninnie and my mom (age 6) in Selma, Alabama*

DEDICATION

THERE IS SOMETHING VERY SPECIAL ABOUT THE WOMEN IN MY FAMILY. To the outside world, they are the embodiment of southern women: soft and tough, straightforward and compassionate, emotional yet resilient. To me, they are my role models, friends, entertainment, therapy, sounding boards, and rocks. So I dedicate this book first and foremost to Ninnie, who has loved me unconditionally since the day I was born; to my mom, who always knew I "had a book in me" and who is and will always be my biggest fan; to Aunt Theresa and Aunt Lisa; Allyson and Caitlin; and my own daughters, Irelyn Gray and Bryre Elisabeth Thomson; and my stepdaughter, Ella Noel Blackledge. Thank you for a legacy worth remembering and worth passing along.

I used to think that behind every great woman was only another great woman. Now I realize how important the men are to the strong southern feminine souls in our family. So I also dedicate this book to the men in my life who put up with all of my strong-willed antics and love me much more than they do the food in this book! To Peyton Blackledge, my husband and love of my life, who thinks I can do anything in the world; to Gregg Beck, my dad, who taught me to be a man even though I was a girl; and to my son, Covington Hunt Thomson, and step-son, Ashton Blackledge, who both teach me patience, persistence, and the feeling of the tug on your heart that only a boy can have.

I am who I am because of all these people who taught me to love and be loved.

Acknowledgments

I would like to thank the many people in the Smith family who helped me compile these family recipes; it was an impossible task. Also, special thanks to Tony Ivory for his many nights of photo shoots and edits, making the food in this book look as good as it tastes! Many thanks to the scores of people who assisted me with childcare, computer advice, publishing leads, and moral support throughout this journey. Thank you to the many friends, my own Skinny Ninnies, who tested the recipes for me as soon as the requests hit my Facebook status. To Stephen Rampersad, who gave Peyton and me the push to complete this updated version. Last but not least, to all those who spent hard-earned money to own a copy of this book: **It is an honor to be in your kitchen!**

FAMILY PHOTO: *(1963) Heading to England, Ninnie and all her children*

TABLE OF CONTENTS

INTRODUCTION 11

BREAKFAST, BRUNCH, BEVERAGES, AND BREADS 13

Top of the Fridge Cinnamon Buns 14
Sleepover Waffles 16
Chocolate Syrup for Pancakes 17
Christmas Casserole 18
Mullet and Grits 20
Sweet Tea 22
The Family Recipe 23
Real Corn Bread 24
Aunt Christene's Hush Puppies 26
Farm Fresh Breakfast Melt 28
Ninnie's Biscuits 30

SOUPS, SALADS, SANDWICHES, AND STARTERS 33

Gumbo 34
Not So Secret Stew 35
Lisa's Easy Shrimp Bisque 36
Road Trip Pimento Cheese Sandwiches 37
Sunday Soggy Baloney Sammys 38
Apple Mayonnaise Salad 39
Deviled Eggs 40
Smitty's Southern Potato Salad 42
Poor Girl Pear Salad 44
Kristin's Cole Slaw 45
Sweet Vidalia Salad and Dressing 46
Strawberry Pretzel Salad 47
Marlene's Better then Boursin© Cheese Dip 48

MAIN DISHES 51

Home from the Hospital Chicken and Dumplin's 52
Justin's Fried Oysters 54
Ninnie Burgers 56
Deedee's Tostidees 57
Grandchild's Fried Chicken 58
Recession Pork Chop & Rice Casserole 60
Hungry Jack 61
Aunt YaYa's Original Ya-Ya! 62
Aunt Ollie's Squirrel and Gravy 64
MaMere's Chicken Pot Pie 66
Aunt Christene's Crab Cakes 67
Steamed Crab 68
Kristin's Crack Pasta 69
Stover's Fried Catfish 70
Big Daddy's Fried Turkey 72
Homecoming Roast and Vegetables 74
Autumn's Easy Roast 75
Walter Gray's Hamburger Steak and Onions 76
Venison Sliders 78
Hey Ma, The Meatloaf! 80

SAUCES, STOCKS, AND MARINADES 83

Perfect Chicken Stock 84
Jezebel Sauce 85
Thanksgiving Gravy 86
Grilled Fish Marinade 87

FRESH FRUITS, VEGGIES, AND OTHER SIDE DELICACIES 89

Scraped Apples 90
Muscadine Jelly 92
Jan's Apple Relish 94
Peaches n' Syrup 95
Apple Cheese Casserole 96
Peyton's Crock Pot Hash brown Heaven 97
Puttin' Up Peas 98
Fried Okra 100
Fresh Corn 102
Blakely Beer Boiled Peanuts 104
The Vegetable Mountain 106
Turnips or Collards 108
Green Bean Casserole 109
Positive Contribution Mashed Potatoes 110
Home Fries 111
Creamy Potatoes 112
Candied Yams 113
Sweet Potato Casserole 114
The Dressin' 115
Smitty's Macaroni and Cheese 116

DESSERTS 119

Fruitcake Cookies 120
Pecan Tassies 121
Hot Mama's Knock You Neked Double Chocolate Chip Cookies . 122
Apple Crisp 124
Southern Comfort Blackberry Cobbler 125
Fruit Bubbly 126
Sweet Potato Pie 127
Double Cousin Bert's Perfect Pecan Pie 128
Second Best Banana Pudding 130
Jan's Lemon Meringue Birthday Pie 132
Striped Chocolate Delight or Methodist Dessert 134
Playgroup Peanut Butter Balls 135
Fudge Off First Place Fudge 136
Tight Lip's German Chocolate Cake 138

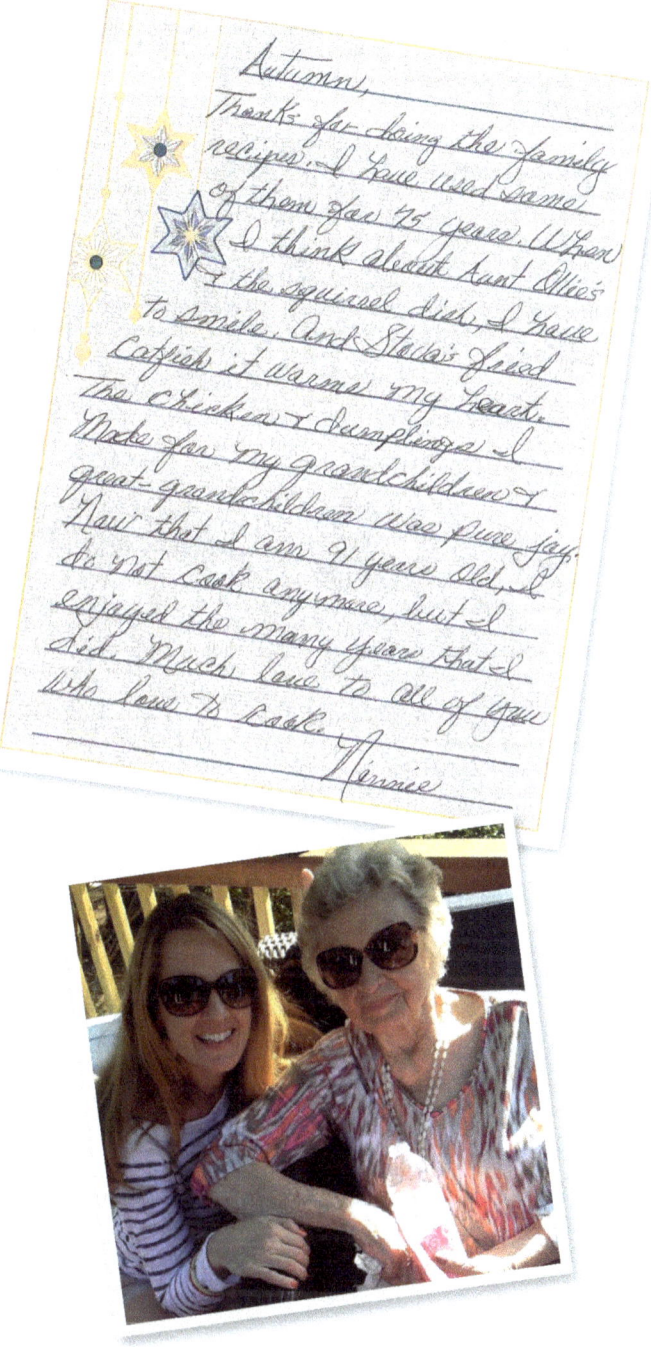

Introduction

FAMILY PHOTO: *Mary Eloise Covington Smith*

A LOT HAS CHANGED IN OUR FAMILY SINCE *Skinny Ninnie's Kitchen* WAS FIRST PUBLISHED IN 2010. I married the love of my life, Peyton Blackledge, and my family grew from just me and the children to a huge family of seven (and two dogs). I started my own law practice and find endless adventure and joy in serving my clients and keeping up with my large family. When I wrote this book, I never thought that I would raise more children than Ninnie did, but here I am, following in her footsteps in this way too, with a big family of closely spaced children.

Quite a bit has also changed in our extended family. Justin has three children now and was charmed with the birth of a baby girl, Miss Ingrid Parker Beck. In 2015 Ninnie sold the home that she had lived in on Lowell Lane for more than forty years, the one with the secret hideout under the stairs and a rock-lined camellia garden in the backyard, and moved to the posh local retirement village, Azalea Trace. In 2017, grandson Rusty Smith married Brooke and had his first baby, Greyson Smith, who when I first saw him brought unexpected tears to my eyes. With another one on the way, granddaughter Allyson Lassiter is now engaged to be married, and Casey Smith and Caitlin Lassiter are traveling the country; Caitlin, as a traveling RN who spends her free time hiking and traveling the world. Ninnie is 93, spry and healthy, and now the great-grandmother to nine! She is hard to pin down if you want to go see her. Often she has a gala or Skip-Bo floor lunches and events planned on her calendar so far in advance she has a waiting list to go have dinner with her. She still drives, is particular about her clothing and appearance, and complains that the food at Azalea Trace has no flavor (i.e. no salt). Ninnie is still the rock of our family's foundation.

Breakfast, Brunch, Beverages, and Breads

RECIPES IN THIS CHAPTER

Top of the Fridge Cinnamon Buns

Sleepover Waffles

Chocolate Syrup for Pancakes

Christmas Casserole

Mullet and Cheese Grits

Sweet Tea

The Family Recipe

Real Cornbread

Aunt Christene's Hush Puppies

Farm-Fresh Breakfast Melt

Ninnie's Biscuits

YIELDS 8 ROLLS • ESTIMATED PREP TIME: 1 HOUR

TOP OF THE FRIDGE Cinnamon Buns

INGREDIENTS

DOUGH

1/4 oz. yeast

1/2 c. warm water

1/2 c. warm milk

1/3 c. granulated sugar

1/3 c. butter, melted

1 tsp. salt

1 large egg

4 c. all-purpose flour

FILLING

1 stick butter, melted

1 c. dark brown sugar

2–3 tbsp. ground cinnamon

3/4 c. golden raisins (optional)

3/4 c. chopped pecans (optional)

Ninnie usually made these cinnamon buns for dessert instead of breakfast, but they are good no matter what time of day you serve them. The only Smith son, my Uncle Ken, claims these as his particular favorite of Ninnie's recipes. Reportedly, when Uncle Ken was a little boy, probably between about five or six years old, people frequently commented that he looked just like Howdy Doody. He had bright red hair and a face full of freckles, and even his older sister, my mom, admits that he was "the cutest thing you ever saw."

Uncle Ken was "all boy" and frequently in much trouble for his antics. Not only was he notorious for causing mischief, but he was also known as a very poor eater. According to the other Smith children, Ninnie spent a greater part of every day trying to make Ken eat. On days when she prepared these cinnamon rolls, she would try particularly hard to feed him hearty foods since they were so sweet, usually to no avail. When these treats were done, Ninnie would allow each child only one roll after dinner. After he devoured his, Uncle Ken would go to bed still thinking of them.

He recalls, "I would stay awake most of the night hungry for another bite." He reports that he would sneak out of bed and see that the rolls were, as usual, on the top of the fridge right next to the switches. Debating whether the contraband was worth the inevitable spanking the next day, he would pull a chair up to the counter, climb up, and devour one (or maybe two). He would then take care to rearrange them so the missing roll wouldn't be missed.

Of course, Ken would suffer every time, whether from the sweetness of the roll on an empty stomach or from the switching he got if the missing rolls were discovered! He claims they were still worth every consequence he received!

GLAZE

2 c. 10x confectioners' sugar

4 tbsp. warm water

TO PREPARE

Dissolve yeast in warm water in a small bowl or cup. In a separate large bowl, combine milk, sugar, melted butter, salt, egg, and two cups of the flour. Blend until smooth. Add the dissolved yeast to the flour mixture until well blended. Slowly add the two remaining cups of flour. Mix till the dough is smooth and easy to pick up. Knead dough on a floured surface until it bounces back. Place the dough in a greased bowl, cover and place on the top shelf of an unheated oven. On the second oven shelf, place a shallow pan of warm water to assist in the rising process. Allow the dough to rise for approximately one and a half hours, in which time the dough will double in size. After one and a half hours, remove the dough, re-knead the dough a few times, and then return to oven and allow to rise another half hour. Remove the dough and roll out on a lightly floured surface, until half an inch thick. Melt the butter and brush evenly on one side of the rolled out dough. Sprinkle with the brown sugar and cinnamon. Top with optional raisins and/or pecans. After all the toppings have been added, roll the dough away from you, such as you would gift-wrapping paper on a tube, as tightly as possible. Be sure to finish the rolling with the seam facing down. Slice into pinwheels that are about 1–1 1/2 inches wide and place on a greased baking sheet. Ninnie would have used Crisco, but I highly recommend a quick spray of Pam or a Silpat cooking liner. Bake in a preheated 350-degree oven for thirty minutes. While the rolls are baking, in a small bowl, mix together all glaze ingredients and pour over the rolls while they are still warm but not hot.

YIELDS 4 BELGIAN WAFFLES *(depending on iron size)* • ESTIMATED PREP TIME: 10 MINUTES

SLEEPOVER
WAFFLES

INGREDIENTS

3 c. Bisquick

2 c. buttermilk

1 large egg

1 tsp. Madagascar vanilla*

1/4 c. water

Special spice extract, which is available at www.spicesetc.com

Any grandchild who had the privilege of spending the night at Ninnie's house usually awoke to these hot Belgian waffles in the morning. These are very easy, but the special touches make all the difference. Ninnie always served these with spreadable Fleischmann's margarine, making sure each little square on the waffle had a bit of melted butter in it, and Log Cabin maple syrup.

TO PREPARE

Combine all ingredients in a large mixing bowl, and stir until moist. Allow batter to rest while the Belgian waffle iron heats. Spray Pam on iron for easy release, and pour batter evenly over the iron. Cook until brown and crispy.

SERVES 4 • ESTIMATED PREP TIME: 10 MINUTES

CHOCOLATE SYRUP FOR PANCAKES

INGREDIENTS

1 c. granulated sugar

3 tbsp. Hershey's cocoa

1/2 cup water

When I heard that Nin would occasionally make homemade chocolate syrup for pancakes for her children, I immediately felt slighted! No one ever told me it was okay to have chocolate for breakfast! My Aunt Theresa said that what made this syrup even better was the little tin serving pot, which was most likely bought at the commissary, that it was served in. Well, here is the very easy recipe that can make your kids the envy of all their friends.

TO PREPARE

Mix together all ingredients and stir until smooth. Pour over hot pancakes or, better yet, vanilla ice cream.

SERVES 6 • ESTIMATED PREP TIME: 45 MINUTES

CHRISTMAS CASSEROLE

INGREDIENTS

2 1/2 c. garlic croutons

1 lb. ground sausage (or any other meat)

4 large eggs

2 1/4 c. milk

1 can condensed cream of mushroom soup

1 sweet onion, diced

1 (4.5 ounce) can mushrooms, drained and chopped

1 c. shredded sharp cheddar cheese

1 c. shredded Monterey jack cheese

1/4 tsp. dry mustard

This casserole is a more recent addition to the Smith/Beck repertoire. Kristin Scrivner Beck, my sister-in-law, brought us this dish when she married my brother, and it is hands down the best breakfast casserole I have ever eaten. It is a savory mix of ingredients that combine to make the perfect breakfast for Christmas morning. Pop it in the oven while the kids are eyeing their Santa loot, and the hearty dish is just enough to hold you until Christmas dinner is ready. Because it is such a hearty meal, I have baked this for dinner, and a friend of mine even reported adding ground venison instead of sausage to make it even more versatile!

TO PREPARE

Spread croutons on the bottom of a greased 9x13-inch baking dish. Crumble sausage in a heavy skillet and cook over medium heat until browned, stirring occasionally. Drain off any fat and spread sausage over the croutons. In a large bowl, whisk together eggs and milk until well blended. Stir in soup, onions, mushrooms, cheeses, and dry mustard. Pour egg mixture over sausage and croutons. Refrigerate overnight. The next morning, preheat oven to 325 degrees. Bake for 50-55 minutes, or until set and lightly browned on top.

SERVES 4 • ESTIMATED PREP TIME: 30 MINUTES

MULTI...

MULLET AND CHEESE GRITS

INGREDIENTS

2–4 whole mullet

2 c. extra-coarse cornmeal

1 tbsp. salt

1/2 tbsp. pepper

2 tbsp. peanut or vegetable oil

FRIED MULLET

I recently met someone who had this to say about my hometown of Pensacola, Florida: "I have never met anyone from Pensacola who wasn't sort of a character."

I laughed and agreed, still not sure if he meant his statement as an insult or a compliment, but knowing that Pensacola natives would certainly take it as the latter. Pensacola is a beautiful coastal town that is steeped in history, military pride, and southern heritage. The mix of mainstream personalities makes it a very interesting place to grow up and, in turn, produces more than its share of colorful people!

While Pensacola is one of the few places in the country you can find fried mullet on a seafood restaurant menu, though the trend is catching on throughout the south, it is the only place I know of where mullet is a breakfast staple.

In older days, residents of the Pensacola area would wake up before dawn to fish Pensacola Bay for the small treasures. After sunrise, the fishermen would bring the mullet home and fry it up for breakfast. My dad also reports that when he was a little boy, whole mullet could be bought for ten cents a pound anywhere in town. While it is considered traditional breakfast fare in my hometown, it can be found on the menu of any good seafood restaurant in town for lunch or dinner…and it is just as good at that time of day!

TO PREPARE

Begin by preparing the mullet. Assuming the mullet available are the relatively small size, approximately one foot in length, you will begin by scaling the fish thoroughly. You will then remove the heads. Do not remove the skin of the fish, as you will fry the whole fish. If by chance you are using the extra-large mullet that can be purchased at a local seafood market, then you may choose to use just the fillets. Either way, the flavor should be the same. In a small pan, combine cornmeal, salt, and pepper until well mixed. Coat the fish as thickly as possible. In a large skillet over medium-high heat,

heat the oil and carefully add the fish to the pan. Allow to brown on both sides, turning often so the fish is cooked throughout, approximately four minutes on each side. Remove to drip on a paper towel-lined plate to absorb extra oil. Serve with Cheese Grits.

CHEESE GRITS

It is no secret that the only grits that are acceptable in the south are real, old-fashioned hominy grits. The old movie line from *My Cousin Vinny* rings true: "No self-respecting southerner uses instant grits. I take pride in my grits." Of course, you can always go to your local Publix and buy some Quaker brand grits, but for premium hominy grits, you will want to try C & D Mills grits out of Cantonment, Florida. The owners, Clyde and Dorothy Bruton, mill their grits and cornmeal using an antique 1926 Hit and Miss engine. Their grits have been used in high-style restaurants like Commander's Palace in New Orleans and Jackson's in Pensacola. If you have a difficult time finding C & D Mills yellow corn grits, I can also recommend the organic heirloom varieties of grits that are milled out of Columbia, South Carolina, at Anson Mills. The purveyor of this grit mill is committed to preserving the corn varieties that were milled for grits in the Civil War South. And while we are on the topic of cheese grits…never, ever put processed cheese products, like Velveeta, in your cheese grits. Come on, have a little pride!

INGREDIENTS

3 1/2 c. water

1 c. hominy grits

1/4 tsp. salt

2 tbsp. butter

2 c. shredded sharp cheddar cheese

2 tsp. garlic powder

1 tsp. paprika

3 shakes Tabasco (optional)

OPTIONS

I use this same method for all my cheese grits and have had a wonderful response when using white cheddar or Gruyere cheese. Feel free to add any hard cheese to this recipe for variation and as a side dish for almost any supper.

TO PREPARE

In a heavy saucepan, bring water to a boil with one pinch of salt added. Stir in grits and bring back to a boil. Reduce heat to low, cover, and simmer until grits become thick, approximately fifteen to twenty minutes. Remove from heat; stir in salt and butter until butter is melted. Add cheese, garlic powder, paprika, and optional Tabasco sauce. Stir until cheese is completely melted and grits are creamy. If the grits appear to be too thick, a small amount of milk can be added. Serve hot.

YIELDS 4 • ESTIMATED PREP TIME: 30 MINUTES

SWEET TEA

INGREDIENTS

3 Lipton family-size tea bags

5 c. water

1/2 c. sugar

I have no idea why Ninnie's sweet tea tastes better than mine, because I attempt to make it the same way! Perhaps it is that Ninnie always steeped her tea in the same orange Tupperware pitcher, but even though it is not exactly the same as Nin's, it is still the best sweet tea recipe around.

TO PREPARE

Bring water to a boil on stove, remove from heat, and add tea bags. Allow to steep for twenty minutes in the pot. Add sugar, stir, and pour into serving pitcher. Fill to top with cold water and serve over ice.

SERVES 8 • ESTIMATED PREP TIME: 10 MINUTES

INGREDIENTS

1/2 gal. eggnog

1/2 gal. French vanilla ice cream

2 tbsp. nutmeg

2 tbsp. cinnamon

Southern Comfort (as much as you can handle)

THE FAMILY RECIPE

All big families have their share of controversy. Although none of the Smith children like to admit it, there have been holidays where, quite frankly, people just didn't want to be around each other. Well, one Christmas when there was a lot of tension within the family I served an eggnog punch that has now been coined "The Family Recipe." It has especially become a staple at Christmas Eve and other holiday gatherings and always helps ease whatever tension may be brewing!

TO PREPARE

In a large punch bowl, allow ice cream to soften. Pour eggnog over ice cream, and add nutmeg and cinnamon. Stir together until liquid is well mixed and ice cream is integrated well. Add Southern Comfort to the punch, or if you will be serving a crowd of mixed ages, you can add Southern Comfort to each punch cup to suit each person's tolerance for the hard stuff!

SERVES 8 • ESTIMATED PREP TIME: 30 MINUTES

REAL
CORNBREAD

INGREDIENTS

1 c. self-rising flour

1 c. self-rising cornmeal

1 large egg

1 c. buttermilk

1/2 c. milk

2 tbsp. vegetable oil

For my mom's sixtieth birthday, Big Daddy sent Mom and me to the Big Apple. Mom had never been to New York City, and we had a marvelous time shopping, looking at Christmas windows, seeing Broadway shows, and eating our way around town. We struck up conversations with salespeople, taxi cab drivers, and hotel staff and proved that no matter where a southerner goes they take their hospitality along. This was never more true than when we made a new friend on the flight from NYC to Atlanta. As we chatted, the serious conversation of cornbread arose. Michael Nazworth of Atlanta lamented that he had gone all out for his Thanksgiving supper and still didn't know why his cornbread did not turn out well. Mom and I troubleshot the failed attempt repeatedly, and we were also at a loss. He had added enough milk to make the mixture soupy, heated the iron skillet on the stovetop, and cooked it in a hot oven; it appeared that he had done all the right things! Then, with a confused look, we asked what sort of cornmeal and flour he had used; he said, "I use Jiffy mix." Talk about your "Ah-ha" moment! I patted his leg and explained that Jiffy cornbread was not real cornbread, that it was more like a dessert you would pour strawberries over and top with whipped cream. So, if you are like Michael and can't understand why your cornbread doesn't taste at all like your mom or grandmother's, you may want to throw out the mix and try this simple, *real* cornbread!

TO PREPARE

Preheat oven to 450 degrees. In a mixing bowl, combine first four ingredients. Begin to gradually add milk. It will be approximately half a cup, but you must watch to ensure the correct consistency. You want a soupy texture, like a thick cream of chicken soup or bisque. If it is not soupy, add a little more milk. Once you get to the point that you think you may have added too much milk you have actually added the right amount! Put the mixture aside. Like good pancake batter, cornbread tastes a little better if the batter has a chance to rest. Heat a large burner on the stove on high heat and put an iron skillet on top. When the oven is preheated and the skillet is hot, add the vegetable oil to the skillet. The amount of oil may vary depending on the size of the skillet, but it needs to do more than just coat the skillet; it needs to generously coat the skillet and have a little bit on the bottom. When the oil is

hot, but not about to burn, quickly pour the batter into the skillet. It will sizzle and crack, making that nice black bottom on the bread. Put the skillet in the oven. Cook the bread until it rises and is golden on top. Allow it to cool a little in the pan, and then turn it out on a plate.

Serve crumbled at the bottom of a pile of fresh veggies, sliced with a bit of mayonnaise spread on the side, or just the crust with the middle peeled out (my favorite way).

YIELDS 75 • ESTIMATED PREP TIME: 45 MINUTES

AUNT CHRISTENE'S HUSH PUPPIES

INGREDIENTS

2 c. cornmeal

1 c. self-rising flour

2 1/2 large onions, chopped finely

2 small eggs

1/2 can creamed corn

2 c. milk

Peanut or vegetable oil

These are the little nuggets served alongside Uncle Stover's Fried Catfish! Aunt Christene prepared this recipe for huge crowds, and I laughed so hard when I got the recipe from her: it would make 250 hush puppies! I have whittled down the recipe quite a bit, although you will still most likely have batter to freeze or spare!

TO PREPARE

Combine all ingredients in a large bowl. Add additional milk if its too thick; the consistency should resemble a thin cookie dough. You want it thicker than a cake batter but not as thick as biscuit dough. Drop by rounded tablespoonfuls into hot peanut oil, and fry until golden brown. Remove from the oil, and allow to drip on paper towel-lined plates or brown grocery bags if you're feeding a large crowd.

YIELDS 1 SANDWICH • ESTIMATED PREP TIME: 10 MINUTES

Farm-Fresh Breakfast Melt

INGREDIENTS

1 sourdough English muffin (Bay's is my favorite, and you can find them in the refrigerated section at Publix near the butter)

1-2 farm-fresh medium-size eggs

2 strips of bacon

One slice of provolone cheese

½- 1 tbsp. Duke's mayonnaise

1 tbsp. lemon aioli spread (I prefer Stonewall Kitchen, but there are lots of brands in grocery stores like Fresh Market.)

Dash of garlic powder

Salt and pepper

Waxed paper

In his semi-retirement, Big Daddy has taken to raising chickens. He built the mack daddy of chicken coops in the back of their property and has raised his chickens to produce delicious farm eggs. My nephews are so used to the dark, delicious orange yolks of Dad's farm eggs that they won't even eat store-bought "yellow eggs." When Dad's chickens are producing at a slower rate, we order our farm eggs from White Oak Pastures in Bluffton, Georgia. We just happened upon this organic farm near our old hunting camp in Blakely and were literally blown away with the flavor of their meats, veggies, and eggs. Before I had an egg from White Oak Pastures, I had never seen double yolks. But the chickens from White Oak are so healthy that double yolks are actually quite common. Now we are quite spoiled by farm eggs, and this is one of my new breakfast favorites. With a fresh English muffin, some Duke's, and a little lemon aioli, this sandwich is perfect for a gourmet taste that is easy to take with you. The perfect thing to send with Peyton when he leaves for the fire station in the morning.

TO PREPARE

Even though I typically prefer over-easy eggs, his sandwich gets a little messy if the eggs are too runny, so I recommend over-medium or lightly scrambled eggs. Open or cut the English muffin and lightly toast it. While toasting and preparing, cook your bacon. It's not very southern of me, but I microwave my bacon so it is very crispy and not very greasy. Once the muffin has been lightly toasted, spread one side with a little bit of Duke's mayonnaise and the other side with the lemon aioli spread. Sprinkle garlic powder lightly on both sides. On the mayonnaise side, break your bacon up into pieces so that the bacon covers the muffin but does not hang over. Be sure to keep these halves on the waxed paper, and use enough waxed paper to wrap the whole sandwich when it's complete.

Tear one slice of provolone cheese in half and lay one half of the cheese on top of the bacon. Put the other half directly on the aioli. Prepare the eggs, and salt and pepper to taste. Stack the muffin with the eggs, close the sandwich, and tightly wrap it with waxed paper. Then place the muffin in the microwave for approximately 10-15 seconds, depending on the strength of your microwave, and allow the cheese to melt. Cut in half and enjoy!

YIELDS 6 BISCUITS • ESTIMATED PREP TIME: 30 MINUTES

NINNIE'S BISCUITS

INGREDIENTS

2 c. Martha White self-rising flour

1/2 c. Crisco shortening

1 c. buttermilk

1 tbsp. butter, melted

Call me a product of the quick-serve 1980s, but I always thought baking homemade biscuits would be a time-consuming project that was not worth the time due to the many choices of frozen biscuits out there. When I saw how easy this recipe was, I changed my mind. These light, fluffy treats are the perfect addition to a breakfast or vegetable supper. Pour a little honey or syrup over them to put them right over the top!

TO PREPARE

Mix the flour and shortening, using your hands, until the mixture makes little balls the size of peas. Slowly add the buttermilk and melted butter. Be careful not to overmix, and work quickly so the mixture stays as cold as possible during the rolling and cutting process. "Roll out" on a lightly floured surface with floured hands. Use the top of a glass to cut out the biscuits, or a circular cookie cutter if one is handy. Place biscuits in a round pie pan that has been lightly sprayed with Pam cooking spray. Bake at 375 degrees until golden brown. Place a small pat of butter on each biscuit when they first come out of the oven, and allow it to melt before serving.

Soups, Salads, Sandwiches, and Starters

RECIPES IN THIS CHAPTER

Gumbo

Not So Secret Stew

Lisa's Easy Shrimp Bisque

Road Trip Pimento Cheese Sandwiches

Sunday Soggy Baloney Sammys

Apple-Mayo Salad

Deviled Eggs

Smitty's Southern Potato Salad

Poor Girl Pear Salad

Kristin's Cole Slaw

Sweet Vidalia Salad and Dressing

Strawberry-Pretzel Salad

Marlene's Better than Boursin© Cheese Dip

SERVES 10-12 • ESTIMATED PREP TIME: 2 1/2 HOURS

Gumbo

INGREDIENTS

Bacon grease or oil

2 (14.5 oz.) cans diced tomatoes

1 big green bell pepper, diced

2 big onions, diced

1 large bag frozen cut okra

1 box chicken stock

Shrimp stock

1 whole garlic, peeled and pressed

2 tbsp. seafood seasoning

1 tbsp. liquid crab boil

1/2–1 lb. shrimp

1/2–1 lb. turkey or chicken meat

1/2–1 lb. oysters

1/2 lb. crab meat

1/2 lb. sausage, either Andouille or traditional pork depending on personal preference

This gumbo is not too spicy right out of the pot, which makes it a crowd-pleaser. In recent years, we have asked Ninnie to make this gumbo for our Christmas Eve lunch. If you like it as hot as Big Daddy and me, you will need to add Tabasco to your serving! To make this gumbo even more delectable, be sure to serve it over creamy hominy grits instead of rice. As my Uncle Ken pointed out, rice is Asian, grits are southern. Trust me: this IS the best gumbo you have ever eaten, and I would put it nose to nose with any New Orleans chef's own brew!

TO PREPARE

Begin by preparing the meat. Peel the shrimp and set aside, saving the shells. In a small pot, cover the shells with water, and boil to create a shrimp stock. If using turkey or chicken, boil or roast and then remove the meat from the bone in long, shredded pieces. Oysters and crab meat should be ready to go once shucked or peeled. Sausage should be lightly browned.

Prepare the vegetables. Sauté the bell peppers and onions in butter until the onions are translucent. Remove and set aside. Then sauté the okra separately in butter just until it softens. Set aside.

Prepare the roué. In a large iron skillet over medium or low heat, add a generous amount of bacon grease or vegetable oil. Add self-rising flour just until it makes a paste, or roué. Slowly stir until the mixture turns the color of a copper penny. Add the tomatoes, stirring until they are integrated well. Transfer the mixture to a large stock pot. Slowly add the chicken and shrimp stock, alternating until the right amount of liquid has been added to create a soupy consistency. Add the seafood seasoning, bay leaf, and liquid shrimp boil. Add the bell peppers, onions, okra, and garlic. Add the meats. Allow to simmer over medium-low heat until ready to serve. The longer it simmers, the better the flavor will be. Prior to serving add salt, pepper, and Tabasco to taste. Serve over hominy grits.

SERVES 4-6 • ESTIMATED PREP TIME: 45 MINUTES

NOT SO SECRET STEW

INGREDIENTS

1 pkg. McCormick beef stew seasoning mix

2 lb. roast, cut into two-inch pieces

3 tbsp. self-rising flour

1 tbsp. pepper

2 tbsp. oil

3 c. beef broth

4–6 Idaho potatoes, peeled and quartered

4–6 carrots, sliced into 1/2-inch discs

1 large yellow onion, cut into eighths

2 stalks celery, chopped

I had to laugh a little when I heard that this recipe was mentioned as a family favorite so often, because it is nothing more than a stew mix recipe, with just a few tweaks and loads more vegetables!

TO PREPARE

Choose a roast with a good amount of marbling (a.k.a. "fat") and cut into two-inch stew-size pieces. In a Ziploc bag, combine the self-rising flour and pepper. Add the meat to the bag, and shake until each piece is well coated. In a large, deep iron pot or Dutch oven, heat the oil over medium-high heat and brown the meat. Add the beef broth and stew seasoning, and bring to a boil. Reduce the heat and allow to simmer on low for one hour. Add the vegetables and continue to simmer for one hour. Serve over white rice.

SERVES 8-10 • ESTIMATED PREP TIME: 30 MINUTES

LISA'S EASY SHRIMP BISQUE

INGREDIENTS

1 lb. cooked shrimp

1 stick butter

1 bunch green onions, chopped

1 c. half-and-half

2 cans creamed corn

2 cans cream of potato soup

2 c. liquid crab boil

Salt and pepper

Zatarain's Creole seasoning

My Aunt Lisa was probably the first one in the family to introduce any "new" recipes to our family gatherings. Our family is not only a bit "clannish" but also set in our ways quite a bit when it comes to food. One Christmas Eve, Lisa prepared a wonderful standing rib roast and served this amazing shrimp bisque as an appetizer. I was shocked to find out how easy this decadent soup was to prepare.

TO PREPARE

Melt butter in a large saucepan. Add chopped onions and sauté until translucent. Add corn, soup, and half-and-half. While stirring, heat the mixture until it almost reaches the boiling point, as evidenced by the small bubbles that form on the sides of the pot. Add shrimp and liquid crab boil. Reduce heat to low and continue to simmer until thoroughly heated. Add salt, pepper, and Zatarain's seasoning to taste. Serve with French bread.

SERVES 6 • ESTIMATED PREP TIME: 5 MINUTES

INGREDIENTS

4 oz. jar pimentos, drained

1 lb. sharp cheddar cheese, shredded

1 1/2 c. mayonnaise

1 loaf white bread

ROAD TRIP PIMENTO CHEESE SANDWICHES

Sunday afternoons after church were usually spent doing one of two things in the Smith household: taking a nap while watching football on TV (Walter Gray) or riding around in the car on a Sunday drive. On those Sunday drive days, the car was loaded with the four children and a picnic dinner. The most vivid memories of these drives come from when the clan was living in Selma, Alabama. Typically, after cruising the countryside toward Chawba, the old capital city of Alabama, the family would cross a particular stream that flowed over the road and stop at a nearby grassy area surrounded with large, mossy oak trees. After an old quilt was spread on the ground, out came these pimento cheese sandwiches along with Sunday Soggy Baloney Sammys (recipe on following page), which had been wrapped in waxed paper. The sandwiches were served with Ritz crackers spread with peanut butter, Campbell's Pork 'n' Beans, and cold bottles of Coca-Cola picked up on the way.

TO PREPARE

Mix the first three ingredients well until moist. If additional moistness is desired, add additional mayonnaise. Spread generously on white bread. Slice and wrap in waxed paper.

YIELDS 2-8 • ESTIMATED PREP TIME: 2 MINUTES EACH

SUNDAY SOGGY BOLOGNA SAMMYS

INGREDIENTS

2 slices Smith's white bread

Kraft real mayonnaise

1 piece leaf lettuce

1 or 2 slices ripe tomato

1 slice Oscar Meyer bologna

On Sundays in Colorado Springs, the Smith family would pack a lunch and picnic at Cripple Creek. The soggy bologna sandwiches are the most predominant memory of the children. "They were so good—I loved them" says Aunt Lisa when asked. The Smith girls also report that, in order to achieve the most authentic taste, the sandwiches should be made as far ahead of time as possible so that they reach their maximum sogginess by serving time! The Smith children also report that they were transported in a Tupperware cake saver and served with cold pork 'n' beans, straight from the can. Apparently, Walter Gray would also eat them with a can of Vienna sausages!

TO PREPARE

Take each slice of bread and spread mayo generously on one side of each piece. Stack the bologna, lettuce, and then tomato on the first slice, and then cover with the other slice. The order is important so that the bologna is on one side and the tomato is on the other. Wrap in waxed paper and refrigerate prior to departure.

SERVES 6-8 • ESTIMATED PREP TIME: 30 MINUTES

Apple-Mayo Salad

INGREDIENTS

4 unpeeled Red Delicious apples, chopped into small pieces

3/4 c. raisins

1/2 c. mayonnaise*

*Nin used Kraft mayo for this recipe.

I must admit that I have mixed emotions about this salad. Despite my love of mayonnaise, somehow apples and mayonnaise just don't attract my taste buds. But every time this salad is served at a family function it is gobbled up. So…the proof is in the pudding, I guess!

TO PREPARE

Combine all ingredients and serve chilled.

YIELDS 24 • ESTIMATED PREP TIME: 20 MINUTES

DEVILED EGGS

INGREDIENTS

12 large eggs, hard-boiled

3/4 c. Duke's mayonnaise

3 tbsp. yellow mustard

1/2 tbsp. garlic powder

1/2 tbsp. onion powder

1/4 tsp. paprika

3/4 tsp. salt

1/2 tsp. pepper

5 shakes Tabasco

2 tbsp. sweet relish (optional)

There is nothing in the world like deviled eggs on Easter Sunday in the South. They are absolutely one of my favorite foods. Big Daddy and I often eat them before they are even placed on the dish to serve, and both of us could probably eat our weight in these little delicacies. The secret is in the use of Duke's mayonnaise, which brings out the other flavors perfectly.

TO PREPARE

After the boiled eggs have completely cooled, peel and slice them vertically. Remove the boiled yoke from each egg and set aside. In a separate bowl, mash the egg yolks with a fork until crumbly. Add the rest of the ingredients, mixing with the fork until smooth and creamy but not overworked. Transfer the mixture to a Ziploc bag. Use the sandwich bag as a makeshift piping bag by squeezing the mixture to one end and clipping the tip with scissors. Pipe the mixture neatly into each egg as generously as possible, while ensuring that the filling does not run over the sides of the eggs. Serve well chilled.

SERVES 8-10 • ESTIMATED PREP TIME: 20 MINUTES

SMITTY'S SOUTHERN POTATO SALAD

INGREDIENTS

6 large Idaho or Yukon Gold potatoes

1 large hard-boiled egg, chopped

1 large sweet onion, diced

2 c. Duke's mayonnaise

3 tbsp. yellow mustard

1/2 c. sweet pickle relish

Salt and pepper to taste

My grandfather Walter Gray Smith (a.k.a. "Smitty") died before I was born but left a legacy of food in his own right. As a dietician in the U.S. Air Force, he was in command of many a base mess hall. What I love most about his mess hall recipes is that they embody southern comfort food, something the "boys" serving in the military could all use an extra helping of!
I have been making this potato salad since I was a little girl. In fact, when it came time to write down the recipe, I was at a complete loss on where to start. I have been making this by "sight" for decades! After much trial and error, I was able to get the correct measurements for this absolutely wonderful, traditional yellow mustard potato salad.

TO PREPARE

Hard-boil the egg and cool. Set aside the yolk, and cut the egg white into small pieces. Peel potatoes and chop into bite-size pieces, approximately two inches each; boil until tender. Drain and set aside. In a separate bowl, combine egg yolk, mayonnaise, mustard, relish, and salt and pepper until smooth. Stir in egg whites and onion. Pour over potatoes, making sure each bite is well covered. Serve well chilled.

SERVES 4 • ESTIMATED PREP TIME: 5 MINUTES

POOR GIRL PEAR SALAD

INGREDIENTS

1 can pear halves in water

Kraft real mayonnaise

Mild cheddar cheese, shredded

Not too long ago, I had dinner with a wonderful friend, and we started talking about some of the strange but wonderful foods we remember from our childhoods. We both laughed when we discovered that we had both been served this very odd "pear salad"! Although the combination of mayonnaise and fruit seems very strange, these individual little salads are mouthwatering! My dear friend and I both had frugal mamas, and we know that this recipe was served because it was deemed healthy and cheap by our mothers!

TO PREPARE

Place the pear halves with the cored side up on a plate. In the center of each pear half, place one dollop of mayonnaise. Sprinkle with cheddar cheese. Voila! Serve chilled.

SERVES 10-12 • ESTIMATED PREP TIME: 15 MINUTES

KRISTIN'S COLESLAW

INGREDIENTS

2 bags coleslaw mix

3/4 c. blue cheese crumbles

4–5 slices pancetta, cubed and cooked (bacon can be substituted if necessary)

1 bunch green onions, sliced

1/4 c. apple cider vinegar

1 c. vegetable oil

2 tsp. garlic power

1/2 c. Dijon mustard

This coleslaw is a very non-traditional slaw that goes great with everything! It has become one of Big Daddy's favorites!

TO PREPARE

Mix together vinegar, vegetable oil, garlic powder, and mustard. Add onions, pancetta, and blue cheese. Toss with the coleslaw mix, and serve chilled.

SERVES 6-8 • ESTIMATED PREP TIME: 15 MINUTES

SWEET VIDALIA SALAD AND DRESSING

INGREDIENTS

SALAD

1 lb. bag sweet baby greens mixed salad

1 c. toasted pine nuts

1 (11 oz.) can mandarin oranges, drained

1 c. sliced strawberries

1 medium Vidalia onion, chopped

1/2 c. crumbled goat, chevre, feta, or gorgonzola cheese, depending on personal preference

DRESSING

1/3 c. cider vinegar

1/2 c. vegetable oil

1/4 c. sugar

1 tsp. salt

1/2 tsp. pepper

1/2 small Vidalia onion, diced

2 tsp. poppy seeds (optional)

I first had a variation of this salad at a friend's house in Tallahassee. It is a much newer recipe, but I have noticed these types of salads popping up across the south, especially during the summer months when Plant City strawberries are fresh and vidalias are perfectly sweet. This salad is the perfect addition to the Original Ya-Ya and other hearty dishes to add a light, fresh taste and a hint of sweetness. We see it lately alongside Easter dinner or summer birthday celebrations.

TO PREPARE

Combine salad ingredients and set aside. In a small bowl, whisk together all the dressing ingredients until well combined. Pour over salad. Serve chilled!

SERVES 10-12 • ESTIMATED PREP TIME: 45 MINUTES

INGREDIENTS

CRUST

2 c. crushed pretzels

3 tbsp. granulated sugar

3/4 c. butter, melted

FILLING

8 oz. cream cheese, softened

1 c. granulated sugar

1 small container Cool Whip*

TOPPING

10 oz. pkg. frozen strawberries, thawed and drained (save juice)

20 oz. can crushed pineapple, drained (save juice)

6 oz. box strawberry Jell-O*

3 c. hot water

Do not use the sugar-free or reduced-sugar variety.

STRAWBERRY–PRETZEL SALAD

My mom, Janice Smith Beck, started making this salad when we attended Gonzalez United Methodist Church. It became a staple at church picnics and covered dishes and is now a tradition in the Smith/Beck family. My mom has always called this a salad, but to me it is good enough to be a dessert. Lately, it is my morning after Thanksgiving or Christmas breakfast!

TO PREPARE

Mix crust ingredients together, and press into a 9x13-inch glass pan. Bake at 350 degrees for seven minutes. Allow to cool.

Mix filling ingredients together, and spread on top of cooked and cooled crust. Chill in fridge for fifteen minutes.

In a bowl, combine strawberries and pineapple. In a separate bowl, dissolve Jell-O in hot water and add reserved juices. Mix together all, and when partially set pour over cream cheese. Cool until completely set and cold. Cut to serve.

SERVES 10-12 • ESTIMATED PREP TIME: 10 MINUTES

MARLENE'S BETTER THAN BOURSIN© CHEESE DIP

INGREDIENTS

8 oz. pkg. cream cheese, softened

3/4–1 stick butter, softened

3/4 tsp. Spice Island fines herbes

3/4 tsp. parsley flakes

3/4 tsp. garlic powder

1–2 tbsp. milk or whipping cream to thin

Marlene Smith is the wife of Double Cousin Bert (whom you can read about in the dessert section), and a friend and neighbor of my mom's. This dip is the hit of many a water aerobics class covered-dish celebration.

TO PREPARE

Mix all and chill overnight to let flavors meld. Bring to room temperature to serve with your favorite crackers.

Main Dishes

RECIPES IN THIS CHAPTER

Home from the Hospital Chicken and Dumplin's

Justin's Fried Oysters

Ninnie Burgers

DeeDee's Tostidees

Grandchild's Fried Chicken

Recession Pork Chop and Rice Casserole

Hungry Jack

Aunt YaYa's Original Ya-Ya!

Aunt Ollie's Squirrel in Gravy

MaMere's Chicken Pot Pie

Aunt Christene's Crab Cakes

Fairhope Steamed Crab

Kristin's Crack Pasta

Stover's Fried Catfish

Big Daddy's Fried Turkey

Homecoming Roast and Vegetables

Autumn's Easy Roast

Walter Gray's Hamburger Steak and Onions

Venison Sliders

Hey Ma, The Meatloaf!

SERVES 6-8 • ESTIMATED PREP TIME: 1 1/2 HOURS

HOME FROM THE HOSPITAL
Chicken & Dumplin's

When I took an informal poll of family members as to what their favorite Ninnie food was, her chicken and dumplin's topped the chart! It was especially a hit with all the male grandchildren. After my first baby, Irelyn Gray, was born, Ninnie was at my little house waiting on us with a fresh pot when we brought her home. Most recently, she brought this dish to Justin and Kristin's house when her fifth great-grandchild, Sheppard Gray, came home from the hospital. This dish is the ultimate comfort food, perfect to greet a new baby or for any other event that necessitates content bellies!

INGREDIENTS

CHICKEN

1 whole chicken*

2 bay leaves

Salt and pepper

Stock from the chicken

DUMPLINGS

1/2 c. shortening

1/2 c. self-rising flour

1 egg

*Free-range is best, and Nin says not to spend your money on tasteless organic!

TO PREPARE

In a large stock pot, place whole chicken and add water, bay leaves, and salt and pepper to taste. Bring to a boil over medium-high heat, and gently boil chicken for sixty minutes, or until it is tender and falling off the bone.

Meanwhile, prepare dumplings. On a flat surface, add flour to shortening until it makes a dough-like consistency (approximately 1/2 cup of flour). Like many breads, weather and humidity can affect the texture of your dumplings, so if it is not doughy enough, you may need to add another tablespoon or so of flour. Add egg to mixture, and knead until the dough springs back. Put the dough to rest in the freezer for thirty minutes.

When the dough has finished resting, remove from the freezer and roll it out on a lightly floured cutting board to about a 1/4-inch thickness, and cut into three-inch long strips. Stack them on a plate as you cut, sprinkling with flour as you go to prevent sticking. When all the dumplings are cut, put the plate back in the freezer while you are preparing chicken. At this point, the chicken should be finished. Remove the skin and discard. Pull meat off the bone in small strips and set aside. Strain broth.

Bring the broth back to a boil, and begin to add dumplings slowly, waiting on each one to rise to the top before adding another. When all the dumplings have been added, turn to low and add back chicken meat slowly. Salt and pepper to taste. Let the concoction sit a little bit, but not too long because "it will all fall apart." Chicken and Dumplin's are best served with collard greens and real cornbread.

SERVES 8-10 • ESTIMATED PREP TIME: 20 MINUTES

JUSTIN'S FRIED OYSTERS

INGREDIENTS

2 containers shucked fresh oysters

1 1/4 c. medium-grit self-rising cornmeal

2 tbsp. Creole seasoning (optional)

Salt

Peanut oil

The ability to fry oysters well is truly a gift from God. Fry them too much, and you lose the taste of the oyster. Fry them too little, and the gritty little things have a slimy texture that just doesn't go down well. Ninnie has the gift. She says there are two keys to success in oyster frying. First, the oysters must be very dry when preparing them; and second, they must only be turned once when frying. Needless to say, you only want the freshest oysters, Apalachicola oysters if possible. Also, be sure to remember the rule of thumb is that the best oysters are harvested in months with an *r* in their names, and the earlier the first frost, the better the oyster! Here is the formula for Justin's favorite fried oysters.

TO PREPARE

Begin by rinsing and patting the oysters dry with a paper towel. In a separate bowl, mix cornmeal and Creole seasoning with a shake of salt. Most likely, the oysters themselves are salty enough to not need much added salt, but it can always be added to taste after frying. Dredge oysters one at a time in mixture, ensuring that every bit of the oyster is well covered. In an iron skillet, heat a generous amount of peanut oil on medium heat. When oil is hot, add oysters to skillet. Watch the heat level to ensure that they are not cooking too quickly, and lower the heat if necessary. Once one side of the oyster is completely browned, flip. Try to flip the oyster only once. When they are done, place on a plate covered with several paper towels to soak up the excess grease. Eat them hot, and be quick because the Becks are hovering!

YIELDS 6 BURGERS • ESTIMATED PREP TIME: 30 MINUTES

NINNIE BURGERS

INGREDIENTS

1 lb. ground beef

1 egg

1 slice white bread

Vegetable oil

Buns*

Iron skillet

Waxed paper

*Bunny Bread makes the softest and best buns for this burger.

Well, we finally come to my personal favorite recipe! These hamburgers got their name because of the distinctive way that Ninnie prepares them that makes them unbelievably juicy. The secret to these great hamburgers is in the grade of beef and waxed paper that she wraps the hot burger and bun in before serving. You must start with fresh, cheap ground beef. As Ninnie says, "You don't want that expensive stuff; you need the fat to get the flavor." I use what Publix calls the ground chuck. Homemade fries complete this perfect casual supper.

TO PREPARE

In a large bowl, allow ground beef to warm up to room temperature. Add egg and crumble one slice of white bread that has been soaked in water and "rung out" (yes, a piece of wet bread). Mix ingredients together well with your hands. Form approximately six burgers out of the combination by evenly distributing the meat, rolling it into a tight ball, and pressing flat. In iron skillet, heat vegetable oil at medium-high heat, and preheat oven to 250 degrees. Fry hamburgers until done on both sides. Flipping should be minimal. Burgers need to be completely done, but not a minute overdone. When cooked through, remove burger from grease and place immediately on hamburger buns. Wrap tightly in waxed paper and place in warm oven until all burgers are done and rest of the meal is ready to eat. A slice of American cheese can be added if desired when removed from heat. Serve in waxed paper. Have all traditional condiments and toppings available, but these burgers are best with only Kraft mayonnaise and sliced sweet onions.

SERVES 4-6 • ESTIMATED PREP TIME: 30 MINUTES

DEEDEE'S TOSTIDEES
(A.K.A. "TACO/TOSTADA MEAT")

INGREDIENTS

1 lb. ground beef

1 tbsp. vegetable oil

1 pkg. Old El Paso taco seasoning

1/4 (16 oz.) jar Old El Paso mild salsa

1/4–1/2 c. water

Tostada shells

This is one of the favorite dishes of Theresa Smith Friday's, a.k.a. "Aunt DeeDee." Frequently, Aunt DeeDee and her husband, Philip, will spend a day working in the yard and doing projects for Ninnie, and she always prepares them this lunch. It is such comfort food for Theresa that she also chose it as her homecoming meal after her long trip to China a couple of years back. This is a great, quick meal, especially for a busy family like my own.

TO PREPARE

In a heavy skillet, heat vegetable oil over medium heat. Add ground beef, stirring until browned. Add taco seasoning, mild salsa, and water. Keep stirring and cooking over medium-low heat until it is thick and juicy. Serve on heated tostada shells in this precise order: shell, refried beans, taco meat, shredded lettuce, chopped tomatoes, shredded cheddar cheese, and a little taco sauce.

SERVES 6-8 • ESTIMATED PREP TIME: 30 MINUTES

GRANDCHILD'S FRIED CHICKEN

INGREDIENTS

1 dz. chicken legs and 1 chicken fryer (bone-in)

Self-rising flour

1 c. milk

1 large egg

Salt

Pepper

Vegetable oil

This dish rings in as the most often requested meal by the grandchildren, hands down, but especially grandchildren numbers three through six! Allyson Lassiter, Caitlin Lassiter, Rusty Smith, and Casey Smith all voted it as their favorite! It must have been because every grandchild was able to get a perfectly fried leg when we were at Ninnie's house. Most recently, my middle child, Bryre, asked Ninnie to cook her "chicken on a stick," referring to these crispy chicken legs! This is a simple recipe, but as it goes with all fried chicken, it takes persistence to perfect the crispy crust.

TO PREPARE

Wash and pat dry chicken pieces. Set aside. In a glass pie plate, mix together flour, salt, and pepper. In another glass pie plate, mix egg and milk together. Dredge chicken pieces first in milk egg mixture until well coated. Then dredge in flour mixture. In iron skillet, heat a generous amount of vegetable oil over medium-high heat. When oil is hot, add chicken and cover with iron skillet lid. Flip chicken once when first side is brown. When chicken is cooked through and is crispy and browned, remove from oil and place on paper towel-lined plate. Serve with fresh summer vegetables and mashed potatoes!

SERVES 8 • ESTIMATED PREP TIME: 45 MINUTES

Recession Pork Chop and Rice Casserole

INGREDIENTS

Pork chops (as many as you have)

1 c. self-rising flour

1 c. white rice

1 can condensed cream of mushroom soup

1 scallion

Salt and pepper to taste

This favorite of Lisa Smith Lyons's, a.k.a. "Auntie Lisa," is probably the recipe in the book with the most mystery as to how it was made. Every Smith child recalls the recipe, but there is much confusion over exactly how it was actually made. As a child, Ninnie learned to make the most of what they had available to eat and was frugal and creative in making food stretch. This may be a false assumption, but I picture Nin in the kitchen looking to see how to make a full meal for six people out of a package of four pork chops! I suspect had there been six chops available, the meal would have been Pork Chops and Hash Browns with onions. Hence, I believe that this recipe is probably a successful attempt at stretching ingredients, and in honor of today's economic times, we have a recession-friendly meal. Enjoy!

TO PREPARE

Preheat oven to 250 degrees. Spray a glass casserole pan with Pam for easy cleanup. Cook white rice according to box instructions and according to serving size needed.

Rinse pork chops and pat dry with paper towel. In a glass pie plate, combine flour, salt, and pepper. Dredge each pork chop in the dry mixture. In an iron skillet, heat vegetable oil over medium-high heat and fry pork chops, turning often to prevent burning, until cooked through. Remove chops from grease and allow to cool on a paper towel-lined plate. When the white rice is cooked, al dente, combine with the can of mushroom soup. You want the mixture to be moist but not soupy. If it is necessary to dilute with water in order to cover the rice adequately, do so in half-can amounts, using as little as possible. Chicken broth can also be used to dilute for additional flavor. Add one chopped scallion. When pork chops are cool enough to handle, cut meat off the bone in to smaller pieces. Mix into the rice mixture. Pour mixture into casserole dish and pop into oven. Cook until heated through, and then put oven on warm until ready to serve. This casserole can also be prepared ahead and refrigerated until ready to cook.

As a side note, it occurred to me that this casserole would probably be even better with some shredded white cheddar cheese on top. Just a thought…

SERVES 4 • ESTIMATED PREP TIME: 30 MINUTES

HUNGRY JACK

INGREDIENTS

1 can of flaky biscuits*

1 lb. ground beef

1 can Campbell's Pork 'n' Beans

1 c. barbeque sauce

1/4 c. ketchup

1/4 c. yellow mustard

1/4 c. brown sugar

2 tsp. Worcestershire sauce

2–3 c. shredded cheddar cheese

*Hungry Jack brand is best.

There is no telling what the origins of this recipe are. My mom cooked this when I was little, and it is possible that it came from the biscuit package or a magazine, although my mom has tweaked it over the years. Big Daddy and I love this meal and will still fight you for the biscuits and the cheesiest serving. This is a great "make-ahead" dish and can be assembled and refrigerated for a hot supper later. During baseball season, this dish graced our tabletop often, allowing us to have a family supper despite late nights at the ballpark.

TO PREPARE

In large skillet, brown ground beef and set aside. In casserole dish, combine beef, beans, and next five ingredients. Around edge of casserole dish, line biscuits up side by side, standing up. Cook in preheated oven at 350 degrees until biscuits are slightly browned. Remove casserole and cover with two to three cups of cheese, depending on how much you have on hand and your personal preference. Place back in oven until cheese is thoroughly melted. Serve hot. Just a warning: the bottoms of the biscuits may never fully cook and may be a little bit soggy. We have never figured out how to rectify this problem and actually find that the melted cheese on the undercooked biscuits is part of the delicious charm of this recession-friendly recipe.

YIELDS 8 ROLLS • ESTIMATED PREP TIME: 45 MINUTES

AUNT YAYA'S
Original Ya-Ya!

INGREDIENTS

4 servings hominy grits*

1 lb. shrimp, peeled and deveined

1 lb. bay scallops

4 tbsp. olive oil

1 tbsp. Old Bay seasoning

4 c. sharp cheddar cheese, grated

8 tbsp. butter

1/2 c. heavy whipping cream

1 tbsp. fresh minced garlic

1 large Vidalia or other sweet variety of onion, chopped

2 tsp. paprika

Tabasco

Salt and pepper to taste

*Never use quick grits or instant.

Now that I am an aunt of two precious nephews, I have my own pet name! For some reason, my nephew Hudson started calling me "YaYa," and it has stuck. Don't all southern women want a colorful nickname? This recipe's name was created way back when I first read Rebecca Well's book *The Divine Secrets of the Ya-Ya Sisterhood*. Years ago, I created this recipe and was at a loss for what to call it. "Ya-Ya" came to mind, and it stuck. Years later, The Fish House, a popular restaurant in Pensacola starting serving a very similar dish called "Grits a YaYa." Now, I'm not saying that Chef Jim Shirley stole my name…but it looks a lot like my creation! So, if you want the original, look here. Just sayin'!

TO PREPARE

Prepare four servings of grits according to package instructions. While grits are simmering, melt two tablespoons of butter and olive oil in heavy skillet over medium-high heat. When melted, sauté onions until translucent. Lower heat to medium and add garlic. Cook onions and garlic until onions are caramelized. Remove from pan and set aside. Return skillet to the heat. Add two more tablespoons of butter and olive oil to skillet, and heat until melted on medium heat. Prepare shrimp and scallops for sautéing by tossing with tablespoon of Old Bay seasoning, and then add to skillet. Sauté seafood until cooked through but not overdone. Remove from heat and set aside.

Once grits are cooked thoroughly, add four tablespoons of butter, heavy whipping cream, and paprika to grits. Gradually add the cheddar cheese, stirring thoroughly until creamy and completely melted. Add a few shakes of Tabasco to grits. I usually add four to six shakes for a family meal where I want to keep the heat down, but more is certainly great. You at least need two shakes in this to bring out the flavor of the cheddar. Salt and pepper to taste. Pour and spread grits into a separate baking dish, and add seafood and onions, mixing until combined well.

It is optional to cover the dish with shredded cheddar cheese and bake until the cheese is melted. Otherwise, it can be served as is.

This dish is very amenable to changes and tweaks. For example, any seafood can be used in the dish. Additionally, a bell pepper or Rotel tomatoes can be used along with the onions for the vegetable portion. If you don't like heavy cream or don't have any on hand, feel free to substitute with milk or half-and-half. I have also used sour cream in place of the whipping cream for a very rich flavor. Have fun with this recipe, and change it up to reflect the needs of your family or friends!

SERVES 8 • ESTIMATED PREP TIME: 30 MINUTES; 45 IF YOU KILL YOUR OWN SQUIRREL

AUNT OLLIE'S Squirrel in Gravy

INGREDIENTS

A batch of freshly killed gray squirrels, skinned and cleaned

Flour

Salt and pepper

Bacon grease

1 bag China Doll rice

Okay, y'all. I really had a hard time deciding whether or not to include this recipe in the cookbook. I thought, "Who eats squirrel nowadays anyway, and will my inclusion of this recipe take my charming southern cookbook and place it firmly in the redneck category?" Well, I decided that I just had to include it. Not many people have a recipe for squirrel, and the story is just too funny to leave out. So, as the economy dips and you wonder what you will be eating next week, don't forget you have a recipe for those pesky little rodents outside your door!

In 1973 Ninnie had just added her first son-in-law to the family, my daddy. Big Daddy, as he is now called, is a Pensacola native. That fall Ninnie took the family, including my mamma and daddy, up to her Aunt Ollie's house. While they were there, a successful hunting trip produced dozens of grey squirrels. Aunt Ollie was an old maid and quite accustomed to taking care of herself, and she was quite a good shot. That evening Aunt Ollie prepared the squirrel for supper. They all sat down, blessed the food, and began passing bowls. Newcomer Gregg took a large spoonful of the Squirrel in Gravy. As he put the plate down on the table, everyone could hear something rolling around on his plate. Ninnie, who was seated next to my dad, reached over to his plate, collected the large, round object and replaced it with another spoonful of Squirrel in Gravy. Gregg looked at her in confusion and said, "Eloise, why did you do that?" She answered, "Oh, Gregg, you didn't want that piece." "Yes, I did," he insisted. "No, you didn't," she said knowingly. This went back and forth until Ninnie finally shot at him, "Gregg, that was the squirrel's head!"

As I am sure that a vast majority of the readers of this recipe will never attempt to cook it, I am relaying the recipe exactly as it was written by Aunt Ollie.

TO PREPARE

Dredge the squirrels in a mixture of flour, salt, and pepper. Heat bacon grease up in your iron skillet. Brown it on both sides. Remove from skillet; set inside oven. Heat some bacon grease in the skillet. Sprinkle the rest of your flour into the hot grease so it makes a brown roué. Slowly stir in water, making a fair amount of gravy. Add your fried squirrel to gravy. Cover and simmer it for one hour. Serve with rice.

SERVES 6 • ESTIMATED PREP TIME: 45 MINUTES

MAMERE'S CHICKEN POTPIE

INGREDIENTS

1 whole chicken

1/2 tsp. rosemary

2 bay leaves

1/2 tsp. garlic powder

1 large onion (any variety), quartered with skin left on

4–6 stalks of celery

1 tsp. salt

1 tsp. pepper

5 medium carrots, peeled and chopped into discs

1/4 c. self-rising flour

1 can of English peas

1 pkg. ready-made pie crust

I hear tell that this is the best homemade chicken pot pie around! The secret is in the stock, so *never* cheat on it by using canned or frozen cooked chicken.

TO PREPARE

Cover one whole chicken (minus organs) in large pot and cover with water. Add next seven ingredients and bring to a boil over medium-high heat. Reduce to medium heat and continue boiling for approximately two hours. While chicken is cooking, in another pot, boil carrots until tender and set aside.

Remove chicken from stock and place aside to cool. Once cool enough to handle, remove meat from the bone and set aside. Strain liquid and return to pot over medium-low heat. Slowly whisk in flour a tablespoon at a time until the broth turns into a thick liquid. Turn off heat and add carrots, peas, and chicken.

Pour entire mixture into a large casserole dish and cover with pie crust. Bake at 350 degrees until crust is browned. Serve piping hot!

If you prefer a thicker topping than pie crust, you can also cover this with frozen or homemade biscuits.

YIELDS 10 • ESTIMATED PREP TIME: 45 MINUTES

AUNT CHRISTENE'S
Crab Cakes

INGREDIENTS

1 lb. lump crab meat

2-2 1/2 c. soft bread crumbs

1 large egg

3/4 c. mayonnaise

1/3 c. celery, chopped

1/3 c. green pepper, chopped

1/3 c. onion, chopped

1 tbsp. Old Bay seasoning

1 tbsp. fresh parsley

2 tsp. lemon juice

1 tsp. Worcestershire sauce

1 tsp. prepared mustard

1/4 tsp. pepper

1/8 tsp. hot pepper sauce

Christene Covington is Ninnie's precious sister-in-law. Ninnie and I have something in common in that we both were blessed with wonderfully good brothers. Ninnie's brother, Stover, was a man of integrity and character, and Ninnie was immensely fond of him. His wife, Aunt Christene, is one of Ninnie's best friends. This amazing crab cake recipe is perfect for Gulf Coast crab or the occasional Mobile Bay Jubilee.

TO PREPARE

Mix all the ingredients except crab meat until well combined. Add crab meat. Shape into sixteen small patties, approximately three inches in diameter. Cook in three to four tablespoons of oil over medium heat for four minutes on each side, or until golden brown. Serve with a remoulade or Jezebel Sauce.

2 CRABS PER PERSON • ESTIMATED PREP TIME: 10 MINUTES

FAIRHOPE STEAMED CRAB

INGREDIENTS

Fresh crab (2 per person)

3 tbsp. white vinegar

1 tbsp. salt

When Ninnie was a young wife and mother, vacations were few and far between. However, during the summer of 1956, the family traveled from Selma, Alabama, down to Fairhope. Ninnie's good friend Bernice owned the restaurant "across the street from the hardware store" in Fairhope. The family spent the day playing on the Fairhope Pier and caught dozens of crabs in their crab baskets, using chicken parts as bait. At the end of the day, Bernice took them back to the restaurant and cooked up the fresh Mobile Bay crabs. When it was time to eat, they lined the table with newspaper, emptied the crabs onto the table, and they dug in full force.

TO PREPARE

In a large pot, bring to boil one inch of water. Add vinegar and salt, which make the crab meat easier to pick when eating. Add crabs and cover. Steam for twenty-five to thirty minutes. Cool slightly and serve.

SERVES 6-8 • ESTIMATED PREP TIME: 30 MINUTES

KRISTIN'S CRACK PASTA

Kristin, my lovely, creative sister-in-law, invented this amazing pasta dinner. Her creations in the kitchen are not only unique and tasty, but they are quite addictive. Once, when we were chowing down on this dish, my brother suggested it was as addictive as "crack." Henceforth, it became known as "Crack Pasta"!

INGREDIENTS

- 1 pkg. fusilli or rotini pasta, prepared al dente and drained
- 1 tbsp. olive oil
- 1 lb. Italian turkey sausage links (medium or mild)
- 1 medium sweet onion, chopped
- 4 cloves fresh garlic, chopped
- 1 pint sliced mushrooms
- 1 (14 oz.) can diced tomatoes
- 1/2 lb. fresh mozzarella, cubed
- 1/4 c. fresh basil, shredded
- Salt and pepper
- Parmesan cheese, grated to taste

TO PREPARE

Slice turkey sausage links; brown in olive oil over medium-high heat in a heavy sauté pan until cooked through. Remove sausage from pan and place on a paper towel to drain. Do not pour out remaining drippings from the pan. Add onions, garlic, and mushrooms, and sauté until onions are translucent. Add the can of tomatoes with their juice. Add pasta and sausage to the vegetable mixture. Add basil and cubed mozzarella. Salt and pepper to taste, and top with grated Parmesan cheese. Serve chilled.

SERVES 10-15 • ESTIMATED PREP TIME: 45 MINUTES

STOVER'S FRIED CATFISH

Stover Covington, Ninnie's brother, is still to this day the hardest-working man I have ever met. Aside from his full-time job at Caterpillar, he also catered large company fish fries. For several years, Ninnie would accompany him and Aunt Christene to these events and enjoy herself immensely. This recipe is a much reduced version of his fish fry batter that made him so popular.

INGREDIENTS

10 lb. fresh catfish

1 lb. plain cornmeal

1 c. Creole seasoning

Salt and pepper

TO PREPARE

Combine cornmeal and spices in large bowl. Toss fresh catfish in the meal until well coated. Using a fish fryer, heat peanut oil and deep fry catfish. Serve with Aunt Christene's hush puppies.

SERVES 10-12 • ESTIMATED PREP TIME: 2 HOURS

BIG DADDY'S FRIED TURKEY

INGREDIENTS

10 lb. turkey

1 bottle Tony Cachere's Creole Style Butter Injectable Marinade

1 jar (3.25 oz) Tony Cachere's Original Creole Seasoning

2-3 gallons peanut oil

The fried turkey that Big Daddy experimented with years ago has now become a staple on Thanksgiving Day. No longer does Mom get up at 4:30 a.m. to roast a turkey in the oven. Now Big Daddy serves up the juiciest, most flavorful turkey in the south for our holiday dinners.

TO PREPARE

You will need an outdoor deep fryer for this recipe. To begin, allow turkey to thaw completely. Before preparing the turkey for frying, you will need to determine the amount of frying oil that will be necessary. In order to do this, take the frying pot, place the turkey inside it, and fill with water until turkey is just covered. Remove the turkey and set aside. Measure the water. The amount of water will correspond to the amount of peanut oil you will need. Prepare the turkey by removing giblets and neck and cutting off any excess fat. Wash turkey inside and out with water and dry thoroughly. Once thoroughly dried, begin injecting turkey with Tony Cachere's Creole Style Butter Marinade. Inject the marinade into the breast and thighs, as well as any other available spot, depending on the amount of marinade you prefer. I highly recommend using the entire bottle. After injecting the turkey, begin rubbing the turkey with the Creole seasoning. Repeat as necessary until the coating is as thick as possible and all the spice has been used.

When using a turkey fryer, be sure to read all the directions on your fryer and follow the directions precisely. Outdoor frying can be risky, so use care with operating the fryer.

Pour the peanut oil into the dry frying pot. Attach thermometer to the top edge of the pot. To heat the oil, start with a low flame and slowly adjust the flame to medium-high. Do not raise the flame to full force, as it will heat the oil too quickly and not only could cause the turkey to burn but could injure the cook. Heat the oil approximately twenty minutes until the oil reaches 325 degrees.

When oil is hot and ready, lower the turkey very slowly into the oil using a frying hook. Once the turkey is fully covered, remove the hook. Immediately, the oil will start to cool. Slowly increase the burner force, and bring the temperature of the oil back up to 325 degrees. Do not let the temperature of the oil to deviate from 325 degrees. Keep a close eye on the temperature, and increase or decrease flame to maintain the oil's heat, which will take just a few minutes. Do not leave the pot while cooking. Fry the turkey for three and a half minutes per pound, which should be thirty to thirty-five minutes. Carefully and slowly lift turkey out of the heat using the frying hook. Allow the oil to run out the turkey's cavity. Keep turkey on the hook and place on a large paper towel-lined roasting pan. Allow to cool until a manageable carving temperature is reached. Do not cover the turkey, as it will make the crust soggy. Once cooled, carve and serve!

SERVES 6-8 • ESTIMATED PREP TIME: 1 HOUR

HOMECOMING ROAST AND VEGETABLES

When I was in college at Florida State University, Mom would always prepare roast beef for my return home. I have included two ways to cook this beef: her old-fashioned way and my own personal method for cooking for a busy family. Either way, this is a fabulous meal!

TO PREPARE

Marinate meat with Worcestershire and salt and pepper, the longer the better (up to overnight). The key to this recipe is using the right roasting pan. Mom uses a heavy, round iron Dutch oven. On top of stove, heat olive oil and add roast. Brown both sides of roast over medium-high heat. Remove meat, but keep the Dutch oven on the heat. Add potatoes and brown them quickly on all sides. Remove potatoes but do not drain off oil. Return the roast to pot. Around sides, arrange potatoes and carrots. Top the meat with onions. Cover and roast in a 350-degree oven until meat thermometer reaches desired cook temperature. For medium-well this will be approximately an hour and twenty minutes. The remaining juice can be used for making gravy or just served alongside the roast for some added flavor.

INGREDIENTS

2-3 lb beef roast*

2-3 tbsp. olive oil

4-5 medium potatoes

6 carrots

4 medium onions

1/2 c. Worcestershire

Salt and pepper

Look for one with nice marbling.

SERVES 6-8 • ESTIMATED PREP TIME: 20 MINUTES

AUTUMN'S EASY ROAST

This is my version of roast beef tailored for a busy family. This dish is the perfect choice when you want a hearty meal and would like to do all the cooking in the morning so that, after running kids around to activities after school, dinner is all ready to serve when you get home! Supper is served! Cooking this roast in the Crockpot all day ensures that the meat will be fall-off-the-bone tender.

INGREDIENTS

- 2 lb. beef roast
- 1/2 tsp. pepper
- 2 cloves minced garlic
- 1/2 envelope onion soup mix
- 1/2 c. red wine or 1/4 c. red wine vinegar
- 2 tsp. Worcestershire sauce
- 1 tbsp. beef stock
- 3 carrots, sliced
- 1 large onion, sliced
- 5-6 potatoes
- 4-5 carrots
- 1/2 c. water
- 1/2 c. tomato juice
- 4 carrots, peeled and chopped into large pieces
- 5 large potatoes, peeled and cut into sixths

TO PREPARE

Pour all liquids into a large Crockpot. Add meat to the pot and sprinkle with garlic, salt, and pepper. Arrange potatoes and carrots around edge of meat. Place onions on top of meat and around edges. Cook on low for seven hours.

SERVES 6-8 • ESTIMATED PREP TIME: 30 MINUTES

WALTER GRAY'S
Hamburger Steak & Onions

INGREDIENTS

1 lb. ground hamburger meat for every 3 steaks*

1 slice of bread, moistened with water

1 egg

1 tbsp. Worcestershire sauce

2 tbsp. vegetable oil for frying

1 large yellow onion per steak, thinly sliced

1 c. water

1 tbsp. butter

Salt and pepper to taste

One steak per person

While we have at least three different versions of how often Walter Gray cooked for the family, depending on which family member you ask, there is one thing that is consistent among the stories: his cooking was wonderful! This was one of his dinner staples. It is best served with Ninnie's home fries and a can of creamed corn.

TO PREPARE

In a bowl, combine meat, bread, and egg, using your hands to mix together. Add Worcestershire sauce, salt, and pepper and form thick oval patties. In an iron skillet, heat vegetable oil and fry steaks over medium heat until cooked through, turning once. Remove steaks from skillet and add onions and water. Allow the onions to cook down until tender. Add butter and cook onions until browned. Serve steak topped with the onions.

SERVES 6-8 • ESTIMATED PREP TIME: 30 MINUTES

VENISON SLIDERS

INGREDIENTS

2 lbs. ground venison

1 pkg. Lipton onion soup mix

1/2 c. fine breadcrumbs

1 egg

2 packages of Sister Schubert Dinner Yeast Rolls (found in the frozen section)

Crumbled goat cheese

Pickled onion relish

There were a couple of years at Bollingbrook that we had quite a bit of deer meat, and I was the recipient of many pounds of it. Typically, when I told the kids that it was venison, they acted like they could tell a difference in the taste of it and wanted "real meat" instead. But when I made the venison with this type of setup, on the delicious yeast roll bun, they loved it. The goat cheese, pickled onion relish, and the venison is the combination that makes this so good; but if you have picky eaters, feel free to use any other type of white cheese that you like. Another tip is to put sweet pickle instead of the onion relish. Serve these with homemade French fries, and it will be guaranteed to please.

TO PREPARE

Combine meat, eggs, Lipton soup, and bread crumbs with your hands until they are mixed well, but take care not to overwork the meat. Form into 12-24 slider-size patties. Bake the patties at 350° until cooked to your preferred internal temperature. Set aside.

Bake Sister Schubert's Dinner Yeast Rolls according to package instructions. Spread each yeast roll with Duke's mayonnaise to taste. Top the bottom bun with the venison patty; top with a teaspoonful of pickled onion relish, and top with a generous amount of crumbled goat cheese. Rewarm the entire slider so that it is all toasty and melty inside. Serve with condiments to taste.

SERVES 4-5 • ESTIMATED PREP TIME: 1 HOUR

HEY MA, THE MEATLOAF!

INGREDIENTS

3 lbs. ground beef

2 eggs

1 tbsp. granulated garlic

1 onion, diced

1 c. bread crumbs

Every man grows up thinking his mom was the best cook, and with this recipe, I can certainly understand why Peyton thinks so! This meatloaf is Peyton's favorite and a favorite of all the children as well. This meatloaf recipe comes to us from Linda Bergalowski, Peyton's mom. There is just something about the way all of the spices and seasoning mix together that makes for a very moist and delicious meatloaf. The kids love it with mashed potatoes, of course.

TO PREPARE

Mix all ingredients together with your hands, being careful to mix well but not to overwork the meat. Form into a loaf and bake at 350 degrees until brown all over, usually forty-five minutes. Talk about comfort food!

Sauces, Stocks, and Marinades

RECIPES IN THIS CHAPTER

Perfect Chicken Stock

Jezebel Sauce

Thanksgiving Gravy

Grilled Fish Marinade

YIELDS 4 CUPS • ESTIMATED PREP TIME: 2 HOURS

PERFECT CHICKEN STOCK

Most people would believe that chicken stock is a straightforward thing: a little chicken, a bay leaf, and some salt and pepper and you are good to go. But when my mom makes her stock, the flavor is so rich it adds to any recipe. It is especially good as the base to any soup or creamy chicken dish.

TO PREPARE

In a large stock pot, cover chicken with water and add remaining ingredients. Bring to a boil over high heat. After stock reaches boiling point, reduce heat, cover, and simmer on medium for as long as possible to achieve the greatest flavor. Stock should be rich in color and flavorful. Remove from heat and strain (depending on recipe). Stock can be frozen or used immediately.

INGREDIENTS

Chicken parts, giblets, or whole chicken

1/2 tsp. rosemary

2 bay leaves

1 large onion (any variety), quartered with skin left on

1 tsp. salt

1 tsp. pepper

2 celery stalks (optional)

YIELDS 4 CUPS • ESTIMATED PREP TIME: 10 MINUTES

JEZEBEL SAUCE

INGREDIENTS

1 jar (16-18 oz.) pineapple, peach, or apricot preserves

1 (18 oz.) jar apple jelly

1/3-1/2 c. prepared horseradish

2 tsp. black pepper

This sauce is a lower-Alabama specialty and is served with all sorts of meats. You can find variations of Jezebel Sauce in pretty much any Mobile Bay-area restaurant. Once you taste this sauce, you will immediately know why it is named after the most notorious working woman in history: it is plain sinful!

TO PREPARE

Using a hand mixer or a stand mixer, combine all ingredients and mix on low until well blended. Refrigerate overnight. Can be served as an appetizer when poured over softened cream cheese or used as a dipping sauce for ham, pork, chicken, or blackened fish.

SERVES 12-14 • ESTIMATED PREP TIME: 30 MINUTES

THANKSGIVING GRAVY

INGREDIENTS

4 tbsp. vegetable oil

3 tbsp. self-rising flour

Turkey stock

Liver and gizzards from one turkey, chopped

Salt and pepper

Certainly not my favorite, but when roasting a turkey, it's absolutely necessary over the turkey to rehydrate! For those of you who like homemade giblet gravy, this one is for you!

TO PREPARE

Over medium-high heat, thoroughly heat iron skillet. Depending on the size of the skillet, add four tablespoons of oil, enough to coat the bottom of the skillet, and heat until hot but not sizzling. Add flour by the tablespoonful until a thick paste is made. Constantly push and stir until the paste becomes slightly darker than a copper penny. Add salt and pepper to taste. Gradually pour in turkey stock, stirring constantly, until gravy texture is achieved. Add liver and gizzards to gravy. Nowadays, we leave out the last part, cutting the calories from approximately 900 calories per serving to a mere 700!

YIELDS 1 CUP • ESTIMATED PREP TIME: 10 MINUTES

GRILLED FISH MARINADE

INGREDIENTS

1 stick butter, melted

Juice from 1 lemon

1 tsp. basil

1/2 c. Parmesan cheese

2 tbsp. olive oil

Salt and pepper to taste

This marinade is perfect for freshly caught saltwater fish. It is also delicious on chicken.

TO PREPARE

Mix together and pour over fish. Cover and refrigerate for at least half an hour.

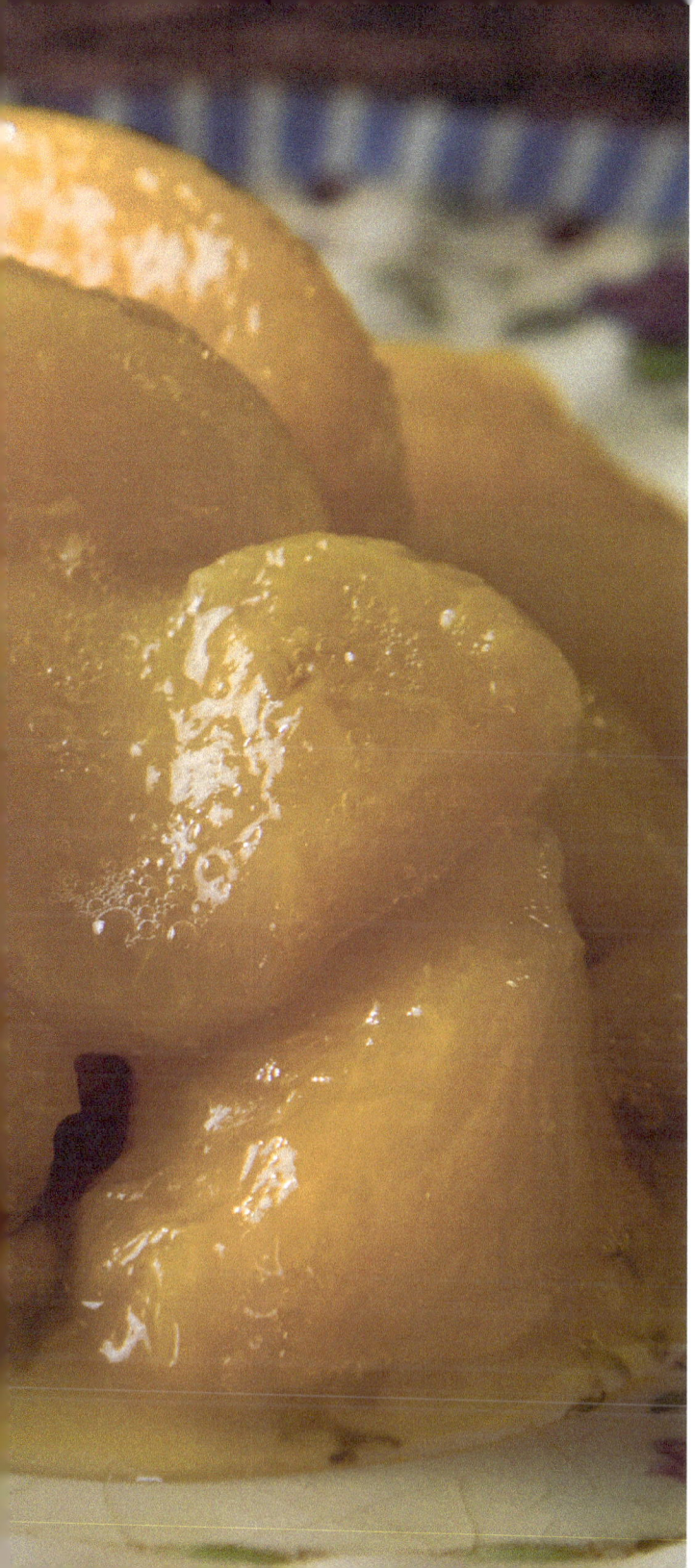

Fresh Fruits and Veggies

RECIPES IN THIS CHAPTER

Scraped Apples

Muscadine Jelly

Jan's Apple Relish

Peaches 'n Syrup

Apple-Cheese Casserole

Peyton's Crockpot Hash Brown Heaven

Puttin' Up Peas

Fried Okra

Fresh Corn

Blakely Beer-Boiled Peanuts

The Vegetable Mountain

Turnips or Collards

Green Bean Casserole

Positive Contribution Mashed Potatoes

Nin's Home Fries

Creamy Potatoes

Candied Yams

Sweet Potato Casserole

The Dressin'

Smitty's Macaroni and Cheese

YIELDS 1 • ESTIMATED PREP TIME: 1 MINUTE

SCRAPED APPLES

INGREDIENTS

1 large apple

1 teaspoon

When talking about this treat with my aunts and uncles, I learned that the Smith children only received this delicacy when they were sick. That fact evidences the difference in treatment between one's children and grandchildren, as I am sure that every Smith grandchild got a scraped apple from Nin anytime there were apples in her house. One of my absolute fondest memories is Ninnie and I swinging on her back porch swing, with my head or feet in her lap, while she sang "Swing Lo" to me and scraped me an apple. I tear up just thinking about it.

TO PREPARE

Slice apple in half vertically. Take teaspoon and slowly scrape the inside of the apple so that it curls up onto the spoon. Spoon-feed each bite, continuing until only a hulled-out apple skin remains.

YIELDS 12 SIX-OUNCE JARS • ESTIMATED PREP TIME: 1 1/2 HOURS

MUSCADINE JELLY

INGREDIENTS

3 1/2 lbs. Muscadine or Scuppernong grapes*

1 c. water

1 package powdered pectin

7 c. granulated sugar

Will produce approximately five cups of juice

When I was young and money was scarce, my mom would think of creative and fun ways to entertain my brother and me over summer vacation. One of the ways was picking fruits and vegetables. Justin and I spent many a summer day picking blackberries, cutting okra, or picking these Muscadine or Scuppernong grapes from local "U Pick" farms. Of course, a Pensacola summer is very hot, and I remember frequently complaining and bragging about what mom considered a creative summer activity for us. As I look back, I am so thankful that she didn't allow us to just zone out to the television, but instead was thoughtful in directing our summer hours. In the fall and winter when we ate this jelly, it certainly seemed worth it to have sweated through our clothes in the 100-degree heat to retrieve these sweet little gems!

TO PREPARE THE JUICE

Wash grapes thoroughly and discard any rotten or dried grapes. In a small bowl, crudely crush the grapes with a pestle or the rounded side of a large spoon. In a heavy saucepan, combine grapes and water and bring to a boil over high heat, stirring so that the grapes will not burn. Reduce heat and simmer on low ten minutes. Strain the juice and discard seeds and skins. Put the juice aside, allowing it to cool and stay at room temperature for twelve hours. After fully cool, strain again through two layers of damp cheesecloth. This is a vital step, as it helps to make the jelly clear.

TO PREPARE THE JELLY JARS

When the juice has sat at room temperature for the required time, you will first need to prepare your canning supplies before making the jelly. For this recipe, I highly recommend the small six-ounce jelly jars manufactured by Ball. You can purchase these jars at Walmart or at your local grocery store. Some people have a specialty canner, but you can do the prep work yourself with no special supplies. Begin by thoroughly cleaning the jars and lids with soap and water. In a large saucepan, place the jars open end down and cover with water. Bring water to a boil, boil for one minute, and then reduce heat. Do the same in a separate saucepan with the lids. There is no need to boil the jar bands. You will need to keep the jars hot until they are filled, so keep the jars and lids in the hot water over low heat until ready to fill. Have tongs and a thick dishtowel available to make handling the hot jars more manageable.

TO PREPARE THE JELLY

Pour five cups of the grape juice into a large pot. Stir in pectin until well blended over high heat; bring to a rolling boil, stirring constantly. While boiling, add sugar, stirring constantly, and allow to boil for one minute. Remove from heat; skim off foam that forms on the top of the juice quickly and carefully using a coffee mug or spoon. Working with one jar at a time, pour liquid into the jelly jar, using an appropriately sized funnel will aid in this process. Allow at least a two-inch headspace from the top of the liquid to the top of the jar, although more space can be allotted if desired. Use a warm, wet towel to clean off the rim and the outside of the jar, and put the rim on the jar. Tighten band around the jar. Return sealed jar to hot water. When all the jars are filled and sealed, bring to a boil for one minute and then turn off heat. Allow jars to sit for five minutes in the warm water. Remove jars, being careful not to tilt or disturb liquid, and towel off. When cooled, check to make sure all seals are tight, label, and store.

*Note: While you can certainly use one variety of grapes for this recipe, the best jelly is a half-and-half mixture of Muscadine and Scuppernong grapes. The combination of the two varieties will produce a pink jelly that is so pretty when canned.

YIELDS 7 1/2 PINTS • ESTIMATED PREP TIME: 2 HOURS

Jan's Apple Relish

INGREDIENTS

4 1/2 c. red apples (approximately 3 lbs.)

1/2 c. water

1/4 c. lemon juice

1/2 c. golden raisins

1 package powdered pectin

5 1/2 c. granulated sugar

1/2 c. chopped pecans (optional)

Red food coloring

This recipe is great for the early fall when apples are everywhere. Tart apples are best for this recipe, which can be canned according to the same directions as in the Muscadine and Scuppernong Jelly recipe. It can also be made fresh if desired without using the pectin. It is a perfect topping for pork tenderloin or chicken, and adds to a hearty fall supper.

TO PREPARE

If canning this recipe (highly recommended), prepare canning supplies and have the jars ready before starting the recipe (see Muscadine Jelly). Core and finely chop apples, leaving on the apple skin. In a large saucepan, combine the apples, water, lemon juice, and raisins. Add pectin, stirring well. Over high heat, stirring constantly, bring to a quick, rolling boil. Stirring constantly, add sugar. Continue to boil for one minute. Add pecans if desired. Remove from heat and add three drops of red food coloring. Skim the foam off the top of the liquid and fill jelly jars. Seal according to the directions on previous page.

SERVES 4 • ESTIMATED PREP TIME: 10 MINUTES

INGREDIENTS

4 c. over-ripe Clayton County peaches (or similarly delectable variety)

1/4 c. of granulated sugar

1 box quart-size freezer bags

PEACHES 'N SYRUP

This simple recipe is one of my own childhood favorites. Everyone who has tasted this simple peach syrup has fallen in love too. The secret to the taste and texture is extremely ripe peaches. The peaches are at their peak flavor in late July or early August. Just when you think you may have to throw them out, you can make this recipe and freeze!

TO PREPARE

Peel and slice ripe peaches. Sprinkle with sugar until each piece is well coated. Fill quart-size Ziploc bags and freeze.

These peaches can be served as a side dish on their own or over ice cream for dessert!

SERVES 8-10 • ESTIMATED PREP TIME: 30 MINUTES

APPLE-CHEESE CASSEROLE

INGREDIENTS

2 cans (20 oz.) sliced apples*

16 oz. Velveeta cheese

1 stick butter

1 c. all-purpose flour

1/4 c. milk

1 c. granulated sugar

Not pie filling

Not too far from my hometown of Pensacola is a little town named Foley. There was a restaurant in Foley called the Gift Horse that was well known for its Apple-Cheese Casserole. It was good, but this version of the same idea is mouth-watering. I make this as a side dish to chicken or pork, and have even had it for breakfast!

TO PREPARE

Melt cheese and butter in the microwave until completely smooth, removing and stirring often. In a separate bowl, combine flour, milk, and sugar. When cheese is thoroughly melted, combine the two mixtures. In a large casserole dish, arrange apples in an even layer. Pour cheese mixture over apples. Preheat oven to 350 degrees, and bake for twenty to thirty minutes, until set and slightly browned on top.

SERVES 8-10 • ESTIMATED PREP TIME: 3 HOURS

Peyton's Crockpot Hash brown Heaven

INGREDIENTS

3 tbsp. butter

1 ½ large sweet onions, diced

3 cloves minced garlic

1 bag (32 oz.) frozen hash brown potatoes

3 c. shredded cheddar cheese

2 c. sour cream

1 (10 3/4 oz.) can condensed cream of chicken soup

2 shakes Tabasco

½ tsp. salt

1 tsp. pepper

Our new Christmas-morning tradition is not only the Christmas casserole but also cinnamon rolls and this cheesy, creamy, fattening Crockpot full of goodness. This is Peyton's favorite, and he and I both eat so much of this we can make our stomachs hurt. This is easy to prepare the night before in your Crockpot, and will cook in the wee hours of the morning while your other breakfast items are baking.

TO PREPARE

In the microwave, melt butter. In a small bowl, mix together garlic, hot sauce, sour cream, and chicken soup. In Crockpot, place hash browns and toss with cheddar cheese and onions. Pour butter mixture on top of hash browns, and simmer in Crockpot for about 1 ½ - 2 hours on high. Stir frequently, being careful not to break up the hash browns.

YIELDS 6 QUART-SIZE SERVINGS • ESTIMATED PREP TIME: 1 HOUR

PUTTIN' UP PEAS

INGREDIENTS

1 bushel fresh peas or beans

Water

1 box quart-size freezer bags

Every summer, the women in my family would "put up" vegetables. I had no idea that this was not a universally known term until I moved to Tallahassee and one day mentioned my intentions to put up some peas. I was regarded with much confusion. But, all my life, I remember sitting on the porch on a hot summer day with my mom and Ninnie (and frequently Aunt Theresa or Lisa) shelling peas and beans and shucking corn, preparing to put them up. We always started outside to shell or shuck, then went indoors to begin the assembly-line blanching—complete with fans to cool the kitchen and blanched vegetables—before filling up Ziploc bags and freezing the vegetables. In hard times, you may want to shell peas and beans yourself, but in a day and age where southern women are busy, multi-tasking people, not to mention have thirty-dollar manicures and acrylic nails, it is often worth the additional cost to buy them shelled. Any pea or bean follows this same method and results in "fresh" summer vegetables all year. I prefer black-eyes and butter beans, but if the white acre or purple hulls are especially juicy, I will put those up too! Bon appetite, y'all!

TO PREPARE

Wash and rinse peas in colander. If you are putting up a bushel of peas, you will not be able to blanch all of them at the same time. Depending on your pot size, you will probably want to do about a quarter of a bushel in each pot. Place peas or beans in a large pot on the stovetop, and fill with enough water to cover peas by about two inches over the top. Bring to a boil over medium-high heat and allow to boil for three minutes. Return the peas to a colander and immediately rinse in cold water, putting ice cubes on the peas so that they cool quickly. Fast cooling is vital so that they do not overcook and sour. Once cooled, in measurements of approximately two to four cups each, place blanched peas into the quart-size freezer bags, removing all the extra air. Lay the bags flat and place in freezer. Spread the bags out as much as possible so that they freeze quickly.

Open in the fall and enjoy fresh peas! Cook them slowly with plenty of water and seasoning. To get the Ninnie flavor, add bacon strips. Add salt and pepper to taste. My modern twist is to skip all additional fats and season with salt, pepper, and a bit of Greek seasoning.

SERVES 4 • ESTIMATED PREP TIME: 20 MINUTES

FRIED OKRA

INGREDIENTS

1 lb. fresh okra

2 tbsp. vegetable oil

1 c. self-rising flour

1 c. fine-grain self-rising cornmeal

2 tbsp. salt

One of my favorite fresh vegetables is fried okra. When I was young, my mom would occasionally fry some for supper. My dad used to work late then, and Mom would store his dinner in the oven on the "warm" setting so he could eat it hot when he got home. On nights she cooked these delectable little nuggets, she would beg me to "leave some for your father." I really did try, and being a good little girl, I usually only reached into the oven for one more piece until it was clear that Dad only had about one teaspoon left. Then I would, with great restraint, stay away from the oven. When Dad got home, I could often hear my mom saying, "Well, we did have okra with dinner, but Autumn ate it all." Sorry, Big Daddy!

TO PREPARE

The key to this recipe is the size of the okra slices and the crustiness of the finished product. Horizontally slice the okra pods into thin, but not thin enough to see through, pieces. In a bowl or large Ziploc bag, combine flour, cornmeal, and salt. Stir or shake until well blended and add okra. Ensure that each piece of okra is well coated.

In an iron skillet, heat vegetable oil on just-under-high heat. When the oil is hot, test it with a drop of water. If it sizzles, it is ready to fry. Place okra into the skillet in a single layer. Try not to turn too often because the oil will get slimy with okra juice. Cook until at least all pieces are browned. However, you want to have some pieces less cooked than others, and some need to be so cooked that they are almost black; the variety creates the complexity of the flavor.

YIELDS 6 QUART-SIZE BAGS • ESTIMATED PREP TIME: 1 1/2 HOURS

Fresh Corn

INGREDIENTS

1 bushel Silver Queen or Silver King corn

1 box quart-size freezer bags

I have only known this corn as "Fresh Corn." When I moved to Tallahassee, I learned that people often termed this variety of corn "Creamed Corn." I was perplexed; the kind of corn I knew as creamed corn was made by Del Monte, was packaged in a can, and was eaten only when you were out of fresh corn or if it wasn't a special-enough occasion to break out the good stuff. In our family, we hoard fresh corn like expensive wine. Now you can hoard your own!

When deciding when the best time to freeze this corn will be, I recommend that you ask around to determine when it is coming in at its sweetest. A good practice is to head to the farmers' market and buy a few ears to test. If it is really sweet, go get a bushel. The timing will most likely be early June, about the tenth of the month. Silver Queen or Silver King are the best varieties for puttin' up corn.

TO PREPARE

You cannot put up good corn if the process for shucking, silking, cutting, and scraping the corn is not followed correctly. Shuck corn and carefully remove silk. To ensure the silk is off, you can use a toothbrush or other kitchen brush and run the ears of corn under water, scrubbing to remove all the silk. With a paring knife, cut just the tops off the corn kernels by running the paring knife away from your body and lengthwise down the corn. You will want to take as little as possible off the ear on the first run, barely grazing the tips and working in long, vertical strokes. After the tips have been cut off, go back around corn and remove the rest of the kernel by cutting down to the ear. Next, take the edge of the paring knife and scrape the ear down vertically until all the corn is removed. On the final pass, you will then scrape the ear to make sure that all the corn milk is removed. You can use your hand to milk the ear completely. Once all the ears are silked and milked, then you are ready to blanch.

Put the corn in large skillets on the stove and cook on low, stirring constantly for approximately three minutes. Remove from heat and use fans to cool the corn as quickly as possible, to avoid spoiling. Fill quart bags and remove all the air. Stack bags in the freezer with room between so that they freeze quickly.

When you are ready to eat the corn, you can thaw in the refrigerator overnight or place directly from the freezer into a heavy sauté pan on the stovetop. Cook over medium-low heat until heated and tender. Depending on the juiciness of the corn when it was put up, you can, at your discretion, add a little milk to the corn and, if you must, some real butter. If you get the corn at the height of the season, you will likely be able to cook without adding anything to it. Remember to ration corn appropriately, making sure that at least one bag of fresh corn survives in the freezer until the following year when it is time to put it up again!

YIELDS A LOT! AS MANY AS YOU CAN FIT IN YOUR POT • ESTIMATED PREP TIME: 3-4 HOURS

BLAKELY BEER-BOILED PEANUTS

INGREDIENTS

Green peanuts

2 bottles or cans of your favorite medium-bodied beer

1/8 cup Crystal hot sauce

1 cup Creole seasoning

1 cup salt

1 cup garlic powder

Blakely, Georgia, was the home of our former hunting camp, lovingly known as Bollingbrook Plantation. Blakely is known for its peanuts, being the home of the largest peanut distributors in the U.S. Every year in March, Blakely has a Peanut Festival in its downtown with crafts, food, and a 5K run. For a couple of years before we sold the camp, Peyton, the kids, and I went to the festival and ran the race. Peyton won his division two years in a row; I guess that makes him the Peanut Run King! Anyway, because Blakely is known for its peanuts, when the peanuts are harvested is a perfect time to get a big bushel of green peanuts to boil! You can freeze them or can them for yummy boiled peanuts all year long.

This recipe came about because we were short on spices one year when I was boiling the nuts, so I decided to add a little dark beer to give it an extra punch. Turned out just simply delicious and much better than you can buy on the side of the road or at your local Circle K.

TO PREPARE

You are going to need a big pot for this, so grab your biggest one, probably the one you use for gumbo or for shrimp. Fill the pot halfway with green peanuts. Poor two bottles of your favorite medium-bodied beer on top of the peanuts. I used Yuengling because it was what was in the fridge, but any rich beer will do. Sprinkle the Creole seasoning, salt, and garlic powder on top of the peanuts. Add hot sauce. Then fill the pot three-quarters full with water and stir. Make sure all of the peanuts are fully covered with water.

Bring to a boil on high and then reduce the heat to medium, cover, and simmer. Every so often check to make sure there is enough water in your pot. You will have to re-add water; make sure it comes up to a boil repeatedly through this process. You may also have to add additional salt or spice depending on how spicy and salty you like them. My crew like them both ways, so I make these beer-boiled peanuts with lots of spice. But you can also make them with just a little bit of beer and salt, and they're also delicious. Just make sure to keep boiling until the peanuts almost fall out of their shells. These peanuts are delicious canned in Mason jars or frozen for use later in the year.

YIELDS 8-10 • ESTIMATED PREP TIME: 2 MINUTES

THE VEGETABLE MOUNTAIN

INGREDIENTS

Black-eyed peas

Butter beans

Fresh corn

Fried okra

1 slice fresh, ripe tomato

This is undoubtedly one of the strangest traditions in the Smith family. Where it started, I have no idea, but it is really good despite its odd and gluttonous exterior!

TO PREPARE

Get a dinner plate. Start piling the ingredients up in the order in which they are listed. The order is imperative so that the juice is sopped up by cornbread and the crispiness of the okra is preserved. Put the amounts you want to eat, carefully creating a mountain of food. Top with the sliced tomato. Drink with sweet tea.

Serving suggestion: I have sometimes seen this with a small dollop of mayonnaise on the top of this mountain, although the person who did that now vehemently denies it!

SERVES 4-6 • ESTIMATED PREP TIME: 45 MINUTES

TURNIPS OR COLLARDS

INGREDIENTS

1 lb. fresh turnip or collard greens

Water

1 small ham hock

2 tbsp. vegetable oil

You love 'em or you hate 'em, but I hear Nin can sure make 'em! The boy grandchildren seem to love these, and so Nin is often seen making a pot to add to whatever meal we are having, just to make the boys happy!

TO PREPARE

Wash greens thoroughly. Break in halves or thirds, depending on your pot size. Add to a large stock pot and cover with water. Bring to boil over medium heat. Add ham hock and vegetable oil. Reduce heat to low and simmer until completely cooked down and tender. Add salt to taste.

SERVES 6 • ESTIMATED PREP TIME: 30 MINUTES

GREEN BEAN CASSEROLE

INGREDIENTS

2 (14.5 oz.) cans green beans

1 (4 oz.) can mushrooms

2 slices crispy bacon, crumbled

1 (10.5 oz.) can cream of mushroom soup

1 c. liquid from beans

1/2 c. grated cheddar cheese

1 can French's fried onion slices

1 can slivered water chestnuts

This is one of those favorite recipes that is served on Thanksgiving and Christmas Day. It is so easy, and the fried onions make it so good, y'all!

TO PREPARE

Drain beans, saving liquid, and place in a large casserole dish. Top beans with mushrooms and crumbled bacon. In a small saucepan over medium heat, cook mushrooms, soup, bean liquid, and cheese until cheese melts. Pour into dish over the beans. Cook in a preheated 350-degree oven for thirty minutes. Remove from oven and sprinkle with crushed onions. Return to oven and heat for an additional five minutes. Serve hot!

POSITIVE CONTRIBUTION
Mashed Potatoes

INGREDIENTS

5 lb. Idaho potatoes

1 c. butter

1 pint sour cream

1/2–1 c. milk

Salt

SERVES 10 • ESTIMATED PREP TIME: 20 MINUTES

Not so jokingly, the women of the family have said that one now-excommunicated member of the Smith clan contributed only three positive things to our family. One of them is this mashed potato recipe. The other two are grandchildren.

TO PREPARE

Peel, wash, quarter, and boil potatoes until tender. Drain well. In a bowl, beat potatoes, butter, and sour cream well with a hand mixer (or, better yet, a stand mixer for even smoother potatoes.) Beat until creamy and there are no lumps in potatoes. Make sure to scrape down sides of the bowl often. Add milk if necessary and as needed. Salt to taste! These are good enough to enjoy without the gravy!

SERVES 8-10 • ESTIMATED PREP TIME: 20 MINUTES

NIN'S HOME FRIES

INGREDIENTS

5 lb. Idaho potatoes, peeled and sliced paper-thin

3 large yellow onions, chopped

1/4 c. vegetable oil

These home fries are a lot like hash browns, but they were never served as a breakfast item in the Smith house. They were typically found alongside Walter Gray's Steak and Onions or Ninnie Burgers.

TO PREPARE

In an iron skillet, heat vegetable oil over medium heat. Add potatoes and onions in a single layer in the skillet. Flip often while frying, not letting potatoes brown too quickly. Remove from heat when onions are tender and potatoes are browned, and place on a paper towel-lined plate to absorb excess oil. Salt and pepper to taste.

SERVES 6-8 • ESTIMATED PREP TIME: 20 MINUTES

CREAMY POTATOES

Apparently, there are only a couple of us grandkids that appreciate this recipe! It probably reminds Ninnie of the Depression and the Smith children of just plain being poor. Allyson and I, however, think this side dish is mmm-mmm good!

INGREDIENTS

3 lbs. small red-skinned potatoes

1/2 c. butter or margarine

4 tbsp. self-rising flour

1/2–1/4 c. water

1 tbsp. pepper

1 tsp. salt

TO PREPARE

Peel and boil potatoes until tender in stock pot. Remove from heat and drain. Return pot to low heat and melt butter. In a separate bowl, mix flour to form a thick liquid, stirring until very smooth and there are no lumps. Add salt and pepper to liquid. Pour over potatoes and serve.

My memory recalls that this was served in my very young years with liver and onions as a special treat for my dad.

SERVES 12 • ESTIMATED PREP TIME: 1 1/2 HOURS

CANDIED YAMS

INGREDIENTS

5 lbs. sweet potatoes*

4 c. granulated sugar

Juice from one lemon

1/3 c. water

Allow about one per person and get the big ones.

The most important part of the Thanksgiving meal (according to the most learned in our family) is these candied yams! They are so sweet you can skip the sweet potato pie!

TO PREPARE

The day before the holiday meal, wrap potatoes individually in foil and bake in a 350-degree oven until tender. Allow to cool and carefully peel from skin. Slice each sweet potato in half vertically. Spray a huge glass baking pan with Pam. Line the pan with the sweet potatoes with the flat side down in a single layer. In a heavy saucepan over medium heat, combine sugar, lemon juice, and just enough water to make a syrup; heat until sugar is completely melted and the mixture has formed a thick syrup. Pour over potatoes. Bake in a preheated 350-degree oven. Baste the potatoes every thirty minutes and cook for approximately two hours, or until completely tender and almost candy-like consistency. The syrup will completely be absorbed into the potatoes. Do not allow the potatoes to burn or brown, and if necessary, lower heat to ensure there is no burning. Serve alongside all your holiday favorites!

SERVES 6 • ESTIMATED PREP TIME: 1 HOUR

SWEET POTATO CASSEROLE

This is one of Justin's favorite holiday side dishes. The dish is now even better since we have huge, fresh pecans from our own pecan trees at the Beck hunting camp, Bollingbrook Plantation, in Blakely, Georgia.

INGREDIENTS

FILLING

3 c. cooked sweet potatoes

1 c. granulated sugar

1/2 tsp. salt

2 large eggs

1/2 c. milk

1/4 c. melted butter

1 tsp. Madagascar vanilla

TOPPING

1/2 c. light brown sugar

1/2 c. self-rising flour

1/3 c. softened butter

1 c. chopped pecans

TO PREPARE

Preheat oven to 350 degrees.

Prepare filling: In a large bowl or stand mixer bowl, combine first three ingredients and beat on medium speed for one minute. In a separate bowl, combine next four ingredients with a spoon until well blended. Gently fold the sweet potato mixture into the egg mixture. Pour into an eight-by-nine-inch casserole dish and set aside.

Prepare topping: In a small bowl, combine brown sugar, flour, and butter, mixing with your fingers until crumbly. Add pecans to mixture. Gently crumble on the top of the sweet potato mixture, distributing evenly over dish. Bake for thirty-five to forty minutes.

SERVES 16-18 • ESTIMATED PREP TIME: 1 1/2 HOURS

THE DRESSIN'

INGREDIENTS

2 cakes of Real Cornbread, made a day prior and broken into large pieces

2 packages of Pepperidge Farm Cornbread Stuffing

2 bunches of celery, cleaned and silked

2 1/2 lbs of yellow or Vidalia onions, depending on personal preference, chopped

Turkey stock (made from previous year's turkey and frozen)

3 tbsp. salt

3 tbsp. pepper

3 tbsp. poultry seasoning

2 tbsp. thyme

3 tsp. sage

This dressing makes its appearance usually only twice a year. It is so good, moist, and crusty; it's the personal favorite of many family members! Alongside turkey, it is my mom's very favorite meal!

TO PREPARE

In a huge pot, add cornbread and cornbread mix. In large skillet, sauté onions and celery in butter until translucent. Add to cornbread. Gradually add stock into the cornbread mixture until you get a less-than-soupy consistency. The consistency should be like soaked bread, but not liquid. Fold in all remaining ingredients slowly and carefully so that bread does not become mushy or break up too much. After all spices are added, taste the mixture to see if anything needs to be added. If for some reason it does not taste rich enough, usually if the turkey stock was bland initially, melted butter may be poured in for a richer taste. Once desired flavor is achieved, bake in a preheated 300-degree oven for approximately one hour. Keep in warm oven until ready to serve.

SERVES 6 • ESTIMATED PREP TIME: 20 MINUTES

SMITTY'S
Macaroni and Cheese

INGREDIENTS

1 (16 oz.) box elbow macaroni

2 c. shredded mild cheddar cheese

1/2 stick butter

2 tbsp. self-rising flour

1 c. milk

Salt

When I was little, my parents could not afford the very fancy Kraft Macaroni and Cheese that my friends served me for lunch at their house. I always had homemade macaroni and cheese, and while I liked it, I certainly did not appreciate it. This is another of Walter Gray's mess hall recipes and is the perfect side dish to feed a large group on a small budget. Despite its frugal price tag, it is rich and creamy and makes me wonder every time I eat it why I possibly ever wanted the boxed kind!

TO PREPARE

Bring water to a boil and add elbow macaroni. Cook to your desired softness. While macaroni is cooking, melt butter in medium saucepan on medium heat. When it is all melted, add flour by the tablespoonful, stirring with a wooden spoon until it becomes a thick, buttery yellow paste. Slowly add milk, stirring constantly. The milk will slowly become absorbed as it is added. When it reaches a creamy consistency of medium thickness, turn heat down to low and add shredded cheese by the handful, stirring until it is fully melted into the sauce. When all cheese is melted, drain macaroni and pour cheese sauce over. Add salt if necessary.

Serving suggestion: You can bake this macaroni if you desire by spreading in a casserole dish, covering top with more shredded cheese, and baking until the cheese melts. Also note that this cheese sauce can be used to serve over broccoli or other vegetables!

Desserts

RECIPES IN THIS CHAPTER

Fruitcake Cookies

Pecan Tassies

Hot Mama's Knock You Neked Double-Chocolate Chip Cookies

Apple Crisp

Southern Comfort Blackberry Cobbler

Fruit Bubbly

Sweet Potato Pie

Double Cousin Bert's Perfect Pecan Pie

Second-Best Banana Pudding

Jan's Birthday Lemon Meringue Pie

Striped Chocolate Delight (Methodist Dessert)

Playgroup Peanut Butter Balls

Fudge Off First-Place Fudge

Tight Lip's German Chocolate Cake

YIELDS 11 DOZEN • ESTIMATED PREP TIME: 45 MINUTES

FRUITCAKE
COOKIES

INGREDIENTS

1/4 c. butter

1/2 c. brown sugar

2 eggs

1 1/2 tsp. milk

1 1/2 baking soda

1 1/2 c. all-purpose flour

1/4 tsp. nutmeg

1/4 tsp. cinnamon

1/4 tsp. ground cloves

1/4 allspice

4 tsp. orange juice

1 tsp. each of orange, lemon, almond, and vanilla extracts

1/2 lbs. chopped cherries

1/2 c. pineapple, diced

1/2 c. dates, chopped

1 lb. pecans, chopped

Fruitcake has long been the redheaded stepchild of the Christmas season, but these cookies bring fruitcake back to the table! These are my mom's very favorite holiday treat.

TO PREPARE

With a hand beater or stand mixer, combine butter, brown sugar, eggs, milk, baking soda, flour, spices, juice, and extracts together until well blended and creamy. Fold chopped fruits and nuts into mixture. Preheat oven to 325 degrees. On a greased cookie sheet, place a rounded teaspoonful of the mixture with 1/4-inch space between each cookie. Bake for fifteen minutes and cool on a wire rack. Store in a tin to preserve moistness.

YIELDS 4 DOZEN • ESTIMATED PREP TIME: 1 1/2 HOURS

Pecan Tassies

INGREDIENTS

DOUGH

8 oz. cream cheese, softened

1/2 lb. butter, softened

1/8 tsp. salt

2 c. sifted self-rising flour

FILLING

4 large eggs

3 c. light brown sugar, firmly packed

4 tbsp. butter, melted

1 tsp. salt

2 tsp. vanilla

1 1/2 c. pecans, finely chopped

It wasn't long ago that Ninnie came with us to Bollingbrook Plantation in Blakely, Georgia, and helped me and the kids gather pecans. I was so amused to hear that one year she and her children collected pecans and sold them to a local business in order to save money to buy her husband, Walter Gray, a shotgun for Christmas. When she and I gathered at Bollingbrook, we noticed a shared trait: neither of us has an easy time leaving a single pecan on the ground. Well, it is physically impossible to gather every fallen pecan, but Ninnie and I sure tried. The next day, both of us were paying for our persistence. We were both "stove up" in our backs; I was explaining to my kids that I had a "hitch in my giddyup!" Despite our aches and pains, we didn't complain when we both had enough pecans to make these tasty treats!

TO PREPARE

Prepare dough: Mix all dough ingredients with stand mixer with paddle attachment until well blended. Chill in refrigerator for one hour. Remove dough and roll into small balls. Press each ball into a mini-muffin tin until it creates a cup that can be filled with the pecan filling. If a wooden pestle is available, it can be used to spread out the dough in each muffin cup.

Prepare filling: Mix all filling ingredients except pecans until well blended and creamy. Fold in pecans. Place a teaspoonful of filling into each dough-lined muffin cup

Bake in a preheated 325-degree oven for thirty to thirty-five minutes. Cool before removing from the muffin tin.

YIELDS 4 1/2 DOZEN • ESTIMATED PREP TIME: 45 MINUTES

HOT MAMA'S KNOCK YOU NEKED DOUBLE-Chocolate Chip Cookies

Like so many recipes, this one was developed "by accident" when I was desperate for a cookie recipe to bring to a holiday cookie exchange. Taking a traditional chocolate chip cookie, I thought adding a little cocoa would add some flair. Well, after I added that, I decided to add a little chocolate syrup. Anyway, these cookies turned out so chocolaty, well, they just about made all the girls at the cookie exchange want to take their clothes off!

INGREDIENTS

2 1/4 c. self-rising flour

1/2 c. baking cocoa

1 c. softened butter

1 c. firmly packed dark-brown sugar

3/4 c. granulated sugar

2 tsp. Madagascar vanilla

3 tsp. chocolate syrup

2 large eggs

2 c. (12 oz. bag) semisweet chocolate chips

TO PREPARE

Preheat oven to 350 degrees. Combine flour and cocoa in a small bowl. Beat butter, brown sugar, granulated sugar, chocolate syrup, and vanilla extract in a large mixing bowl on medium speed until creamy. Beat in eggs, one at a time, and then beat for two minutes on high, or until light and fluffy. Gradually mix in flour mixture using the dough hook attachment on your mixer, or stir in using a spoon until creamy. Add chocolate chips. Drop by rounded tablespoonfuls onto Silpat-lined or ungreased cookie sheet.

Bake for eleven to thirteen minutes. Cool on baking sheet for two minutes.

SERVES 8-10 • ESTIMATED PREP TIME: 45 MINUTES

APPLE CRISP

INGREDIENTS

5 c. sliced apples

3/4 c. quick-cooking oats

1 c. all purpose flour

1 c. light brown sugar, firmly packed

1/2 tsp. salt

1 tsp. cinnamon

1/2 c. butter, cut into 8 pieces

In the late 1960s, the Smiths were stationed in Colorado Springs, Colorado. One fall Saturday, they visited an apple farm. All the children remember the aroma from the large barn as they walked toward it, and inside saw it almost completely full of red apples. They purchased several boxes of freshly picked apples to take home, and that evening Ninnie made this recipe with the fruit. Aunt Theresa put her hand on her chest remembering the taste of this Apple Crisp, the memory of the flavor was so vivid and fresh.

TO PREPARE

In a large bowl, combine oats, flour, brown sugar, salt, and cinnamon. Add pieces of butter by hand, rubbing the pieces into the mixture until the mixture is crumbly. Butter a 9x13-inch casserole dish and place the sliced apples in single layer. Top with crumbly mixture. Preheat oven to 350 degrees and bake approximately twenty minutes until browned on top. Serve warm over vanilla ice cream.

SERVES 8-10 • ESTIMATED PREP TIME: 45 MINUTES

INGREDIENTS

FILLING

5 c. fresh blackberries, or 2 (14 oz.) packages of frozen berries, thawed and drained

1 c. sugar

4 tbsp. all-purpose flour

1 tbsp. lemon juice

1/2 tsp. Madagascar vanilla

1 tbsp. Southern Comfort bourbon

CRUST

2 tbsp. butter or margarine, melted

1 3/4 c. Bisquick

1/2 c. buttermilk

1/4 c. sugar

SOUTHERN COMFORT
Blackberry Cobbler

This is my own original recipe that is the usual dessert that accompanies a meal taken to a neighbor or friend after a major life event, like the birth of a baby, a move, or a death. Because it can use frozen or fresh berries, it is a little taste of summer all year long.

TO PREPARE

Combine first six ingredients; toss well. Spoon into a lightly greased eight- or nine-inch square pan, or for a richer flavor, a warmed large iron skillet. Set aside. Prepare crust and spoon nine mounds over blackberries. I find it helpful to use an ice cream or batter scoop so the mixture comes out onto the berries easily. Brush with butter and sprinkle with remaining sugar. Bake in a preheated 425-degree oven, uncovered, until browned and bubbly. Serve with ice cream to cut the sweetness. For more flavor, cook in an iron skillet or Dutch oven.

SERVES 4-6 • ESTIMATED PREP TIME: 20 MINUTES

FRUIT BUBBLY

INGREDIENTS

1/2 c. butter

1 c. granulated sugar

1 c. self-rising flour

1 c. milk

1 tsp. vanilla

1/2 tsp. cinnamon

2 lbs. fruit, sliced*

*Any type of fruit will work, although sliced apples, pears, and peaches seem to work best.

When rummaging through my recipes, I located this recipe that was handwritten by my Aunt Theresa. I wish there was a font that resembled it so I could share how unique her writing is. It was on a little sheet of paper from the hospital where she worked. This recipe doesn't have a name on it, but I recall that the finished product resembled a fruit cobbler but was much bubblier!

TO PREPARE

Melt butter in an eight-by-fourteen-inch casserole dish in a preheated 350-degree oven. While butter is melting, combine next five ingredients together. Pour mixture into casserole dish after butter has completely melted, and stir. Place fruit on the top in a single layer. Bake for approximately thirty minutes until golden and bubbly. Serve with homemade whipped cream or ice cream.

SERVES 6-8 • ESTIMATED PREP TIME: 45 MINUTES

SWEET POTATO PIE

INGREDIENTS

2 ready-made pie crusts

2 c. boiled sweet potatoes, drained

2 large eggs

3/4 c. sugar

1 large can evaporated milk

1 tsp. cinnamon

1/4 tsp. cloves

1/2 tsp. ginger

1/2 tsp. salt

2 tbsp. butter, softened, beat with mixer

Sweet potato pie happens to be my dad's favorite dessert. This pie is as easy as it is delicious! This recipe actually makes two pies, which won't go as far as it would seem.

TO PREPARE

For this recipe you will want to use two shallow—not deep-dish—pie plates. Press ready-made piecrusts into pie plate, trimming excess from the edges. Combine all ingredients in a stand mixer bowl or other large mixing bowl. Beat on medium-high speed until creamy. When the mixture is sufficiently creamed, remove bowl but do not scrape off the mixer blades. The mixer blades will naturally remove the strings from the sweet potatoes, and you don't want these in your pie. Divide the pie filling into the two pie plates. Bake in a preheated 350-degree oven for one hour. Cool before serving.

SERVES 6-8 • ESTIMATED PREP TIME: 45 MINUTES

DOUBLE COUSIN BERT'S PERFECT PECAN PIE

INGREDIENTS

1 c. pecans, whole or halves

1 ready-made pie crust

1 egg white

3 well-beaten eggs

1 c. light corn syrup

1/2 c. dark brown sugar

2 tsp. melted butter

2 tsp. 2-Fold Madagascar vanilla

1/4 tsp. salt

When I begin telling people about this cookbook, I never fail to mention this particular recipe. Much like the Squirrel in Gravy recipe, the term "double cousin" elicits much attention and confusion. But in reality, a double cousin is nothing more than a cousin related to you on both sides of a family; most commonly, siblings marry siblings, and the resulting children are double cousins. Double Cousin Bert is a distant cousin who shares four common great-grandparents with my mom, on both the Covington and Smith sides of her family. Bert and his wife, Marlene, live just down the road from Mamma and Big Daddy's house, and they are now also close friends. Besides being one of the most colorful men I have met lately, he is also a master at baking a pecan pie!

TO PREPARE

The secret to this pie is toasting the pecans. Toast pecans by spreading them on an ungreased cookie sheet. Place in a preheated 350-degree oven and heat until you smell the flavor of the pecan, usually four to five minutes. Do not allow them to burn. Remove the pecans, allow to cool, and roughly chop. Pecans need to be toasted before chopped. Set aside.

In a nine-inch pie plate, spread ready-made pie crust evenly. Trim edges of crust so it's not overhanging the edges, and pinch with fingers along the edge. In a bowl, beat the white of one egg and brush all over pie crust. Set aside. Combine eggs, corn syrup, sugar, butter, vanilla, and salt, and mix with hand beater or stand mixer until creamy. Fold in toasted pecans. Pour batter into pie shell, and bake in a preheated 350-degree oven for forty-five minutes. Cool on a wire rack and serve.

SERVES 10-12 • ESTIMATED PREP TIME: 40 MINUTES

SECOND-BEST BANANA PUDDING

INGREDIENTS

2 (8 oz.) boxes Jell-O instant vanilla pudding

4 c. milk

1 capful Madagascar vanilla

8 oz. Philadelphia cream cheese

2 c. heavy whipping cream

1 tsp. granulated sugar

4-5 ripe bananas

1 ½ box vanilla wafers

One jar Smucker's caramel topping

Peyton and I have a favorite restaurant in town called Restaurant Iron. Not only does Iron have the best bartenders in town, who create new and classic fusion cocktails, but Chef Alex McPhail has created unbelievable dishes with creative blends of Southern cuisine and new flavors for unsurpassable taste. Peyton and I may have a little food crush on this place. Chef Alex also happens on occasion to serve his mother's banana pudding recipe in the spring and summer months. It is frankly the best banana pudding I have ever tasted, hands down. If you are ever in Pensacola, you need to try Restaurant Iron and maybe even call ahead and ask for banana pudding to make sure you can taste this. But, if you never make your way here, you can try this, the second-best banana pudding I have ever tasted, to hold you over. I've taken some inspiration from him and tweaked my old recipe a little. Chef Alex also layers his banana pudding in individual-size Mason jars so that you can see every layer of the pudding and also taste every bit of it as you eat it--the perfect presentation for this almost-perfect banana pudding.

TO PREPARE

Prepare instant vanilla pudding according to the instructions on the box, adding one capful of Madagascar vanilla. Set aside. In your stand mixer, whip one package of softened Philadelphia cream cheese. The whipped Philadelphia cream cheese will also work. Once whipped and fluffy, set aside. Also in your stand mixer, beat two cups of heavy whipping cream and one teaspoon of granulated sugar until thick whipped cream forms. Slowly add the whipped cream cheese to this mixture.

Using an 11x13-inch baking dish or individual Mason jars, begin to layer your banana pudding, starting with caramel, followed by vanilla wafers, bananas, and then repeat.

Drizzle caramel topping on the bottom of the pan just slightly, or about a half teaspoon if using the Mason jars. After the caramel first layer, add a single layer of vanilla wafers. Top with sliced bananas, evenly distributed. Spread a layer of the whipped cream filling evenly on top. Drizzle with more caramel topping. Repeat the layers, making sure the top layer is the whipped cream. Use the vanilla wafer crumbs to lightly sprinkle and garnish the top of the cream cheese–whipped cream filling for a decorative finish.

Refrigerate for at least one hour and serve cold.

SERVES 6-8 • ESTIMATED PREP TIME: 45 MINUTES

JAN'S BIRTHDAY LEMON MERINGUE PIE

INGREDIENTS

CRUST

1 1/4 c. all-purpose flour

1/4 tsp. salt

3 tbsp. shortening

3 tbsp. cold butter, cut into bits

2–3 tbsp. cold butter

Ninnie makes this pie, my mom's favorite, for her every year on her birthday, and I do believe that she eats the entire thing by herself! She says that it is "so smooth it is best eaten for breakfast"!

TO PREPARE

PREPARE PIE CRUST

In a medium bowl, combine flour and salt. Mix well. With pastry blender or two knives used scissors-fashion, cut in shortening and butter until mixture resembles coarse crumbs. Sprinkle with water, one tablespoon at a time, tossing with fork until pastry holds together to form a dough.

Shape dough into a 1/2-inch-thick disk; wrap in plastic wrap. Freeze one hour or refrigerate two hours or overnight. If pastry is very cold, let stand a few minutes at room temperature before rolling.

Preheat oven to 450 degrees. On lightly floured surface with lightly floured rolling pin, roll out pastry to thirteen inches around. Place rolling pin across center; lift pastry to drape over rolling pin and transfer to nine-inch pie plate. Press pastry gently to line pan. Trim edges and decoratively pinch.

Line pastry shell with foil and bake twelve minutes or until pastry is set. Reduce oven to 400 degrees. Lift foil and bake an additional six to eight minutes until it is completely done and light brown. Cool.

FILLING

1 1/4 c. sugar

1/2 c. cornstarch

1/4 tsp. salt

2 c. water

4 large egg yolks

1/2 c. fresh lemon juice

4 tbsp. butter, softened

2 tsp. grated lemon zest

MERINGUE

4 large egg whites, at room temperature

1/4 tsp. cream of tartar

1/3 c. sugar

Lemon Filling

In a medium saucepan, combine sugar, cornstarch, and salt, and mix well. Gradually stir in the water until mixture is blended and smooth. Heat to boiling over medium heat, stirring constantly, and boil one minute. Remove from heat.

In a small bowl, whisk egg yolks until blended. Pour in about half a cup of hot cornstarch mixture, whisking until blended. Stir together lemon juice, butter, and lemon zest, and pour into cornstarch mixture. Pour hot mixture into pastry shell and set aside. Preheat oven to 400 degrees. Prepare meringue. In mixer bowl, add egg whites and cream of tartar at medium speed and beat until frothy. Add sugar two tablespoons at a time. When stiff peaks are achieved, spread on top of pie. Bake pie eight to ten minutes until top is browned. Chill in refrigerator and serve.

SERVES 10-12 • ESTIMATED PREP TIME: 30 MINUTES

STRIPED CHOCOLATE
Delight
(Methodist Dessert)

My little brother Justin was a college baseball player. When he first went away to school, the booster organization arranged for each player to have a local host family that provided some additional support for the player, most often feeding them in some way. On one particular occasion, Justin was invited to a pot luck supper at his host family's Methodist church, and he was delighted to find this homey dessert: hence the name "Methodist Dessert."

INGREDIENTS

CRUST

1 1/2 c. graham cracker crumbs

1/4 c. granulated sugar

1/3 c. butter melted

MIDDLE LAYER

8 oz. cream cheese, softened

1/4 c. granulated sugar

2 tbsp. milk

1 1/2 c. Cool Whip

TOP LAYER

2 packages instant chocolate pudding

3 1/2 c. milk

TO PREPARE

Combine all of the crust ingredients until crumbly and press into a nine-by-thirteen-inch pan. Chill fifteen minutes. Prepare middle layer by beating cream cheese, sugar, and milk until smooth. Fold in Cool Whip. Spread onto crust and set aside. Prepare third layer by beating together, with a hand mixer, the pudding mix and milk. Pour over second layer. Chill for two hours or overnight. When ready to serve, spread an additional layer of Cool Whip over the top.

YIELDS 3 DOZEN • ESTIMATED PREP TIME: 30 MINUTES

Playgroup Peanut Butter Balls

INGREDIENTS

1 c. peanut butter

1/2 c. light corn syrup

1/2 c. 10x confectioners' sugar

1/4 c. shredded coconut

2 c. Cheerios

1 c. semisweet chocolate chips

1/2 tsp. Madagascar vanilla or, alternatively, Southern Comfort or Jack Daniels

1 tbsp. shortening

When my oldest daughter, Irelyn, was a baby, I joined a handful of other moms in a playgroup. These peanut butter treats made their debut at a Halloween party for the kids, who were about six to nine months old. Funny thing is, none of the kids were even allowed to eat peanut butter at the time! Needless to say, they were devoured by the moms!

TO PREPARE

Stir together peanut butter, corn syrup, coconut, and sugar. Once combined well, stir in Cheerios. Roll into two-inch balls and set aside. In a small saucepan over low heat, melt chocolate and shortening. Add vanilla or liquor. Remove from heat. Dip balls into chocolate mixture until covered, and set aside on a waxed paper-lined pan to cool.

YIELDS 3 LBS. OR 40 SQUARES • ESTIMATED PREP TIME: 30 MINUTES

FUDGE OFF
FIRST-PLACE FUDGE

INGREDIENTS

2 c. granulated sugar

3/4 c. unsalted butter

2/3 c. evaporated milk, or 1 (5 oz.) can

12 oz. semisweet chocolate chips

1 jar marshmallow cream

1 1/2 tsp. vanilla

A more recent tradition in the extended Smith family is the "Fudge Off." Usually occurring on Christmas Eve, the self-proclaimed fudge masters bring their fudge and the men judge the flavor. Because of its superior texture and smoothness, Aunt DeeDee is the usual winner. While I myself, as well as Auntie Lisa and "the girls," have won once or twice, Theresa still claims the most wins and is the still-reigning fudge champion. Theresa claims that the secret to her success is the willingness to make the top especially smooth, to which Lisa and I will concede but cannot muster enough patience to achieve! No doubt about it, this is the best fudge you will ever eat!

TO PREPARE

You have to move quickly on this recipe, so be sure to set all your ingredients out and open all your ingredients so that they are ready to use in a hurry. In a large saucepan, bring sugar, butter, and milk to a rolling boil on medium-high heat; keep at a rolling boil for five minutes, stirring constantly. Remove from heat.

Stir chocolate chips and marshmallow cream. When creamy, add vanilla. Pour into a 9x13-inch pan. Smooth obsessively with the back of a spoon that has been sprayed with just a little Pam (or a tiny bit of melted butter).

Allow to cool and then cut into one-inch squares. Serve these on a decorative platter or cute tin, and begin bribing men to vote for your confection. Do not fail to point out the obvious smooth top and creamy texture of your creation and blatantly hint as to which one is your submission.

Autumn's addition: I like to sometimes use milk chocolate chips for a change of pace. My dad seems to like it better this way as well.

*Note: In recent years, Lisa and I have discovered the value of high-quality vanilla extract. You must never use the kind made by McCormick and labeled "artificially flavored." Use the good stuff! Lisa buys hers at Williams-Sonoma. I get mine at TJ Maxx for half the price! I also use a little more than a teaspoon because this vanilla is so good you could chug it from the bottle to keep you warm at an Alabama football game.

Tight Lip's German Chocolate Cake

For many years, we have questioned Aunt Deedee's genetic connection to the Smith family. There are many things that make her unique among Smiths, and this recipe is just another example of her uniqueness. You see, the ladies in our family seem to have a hereditary loose-lip problem. If we hear something, we just can't keep it a secret. All my life I've been told things that begin with, "Don't tell so and so I told you, but…" In time, everyone in the family knows the "secret" being passed around like gravy. We all seem to suffer from this calamity. Everyone, that is, except Theresa! Instead, Theresa will declare, "I am not at liberty to say." Well, when I asked for her German Chocolate Cake recipe, here was her response: "I just use the recipe that is on the German chocolate box (the bar of chocolate). Of course, it took thirty years to perfect the process!"

If that is not the most vague response you can give, I am not sure what is. What box? What bar of chocolate? What tricks of perfection?

Alas, the German Chocolate Cake, made best by Aunt DeeDee, will remain a mystery for now. Tight Lips just won't talk! So you'll just have to beg her to bake it for you!

About the Author

Autumn Beck Blackledge is the eldest grandchild in her large southern family, a Pensacola native and graduate of Tate High School and Florida State University and FSU College of Law. While she has been an attorney for over sixteen years, she has also spent time as a stay-at-home mom, a lobbyist for the Florida Chamber of Commerce in Tallahassee, and as a political blogger and amateur political radio commentator. In 2014 Autumn started her own firm focusing on marital and family law. She is consistently reviewed and rated as a top lawyer in publications such as *SuperLawyers, Legal Elite by Florida Trend,* and voted to be on the *Pensacola Powerlist, Best Attorney on the Coast,* as well as other superlatives.

Autumn is married to Peyton Blackledge, a professional firefighter, and together they have five closely spaced children ranging in age from nine to seventeen. At the time of this writing, Ashton Blackledge (17) is a senior at Catholic High School and will likely be joining the U.S. Navy after graduation. The other four children attend Episcopal Day School: Irelyn Thomson (13) will be an eighth-grader; Ella Blackledge (12) will be a seventh-grader; Bryre Thomson (11) will be a sixth-grader; and finally Covington "Cov" Thomson (9) will be a fifth-grader. They are all involved in as many activities as they can find: swimming, volleyball, basketball, cheer, football, and music.

Autumn and Peyton share a love of the community, which they are hoping to pass on to their children by modeling a commitment to the people in their area and to local charities. Autumn has a passion for leadership and serves on the Sacred Heart Foundation Board and the Pensacola Little Theater and Cultural Center Board of Trustees, while Peyton serves on the board for Leaning Post Ranch. Autumn and Peyton also enjoy the local political scene, where they are committed to electing strong local talent to statewide and local positions, so you can often see the family fundraising for politicians and political causes. One of Autumn's most fun political roles is as one of six, and the only female, Charter Masters of the Irish Politicians Club, a private club located at the historic and famous McGuire's Irish Pub, where she gets to wheel and deal for memberships in the selective group, a position that always brings a sly smile to her face.

Autumn is a published author, not only of this humorous cookbook, which reflects her passion for the culinary and societal idiosyncrasies of the American South, but also of a variety of published articles on various family law topics.

www.ingramcontent.com/pod-product-compliance
Lightning Source LLC
Chambersburg PA
CBHW051347110526
44591CB00025B/2936